The Chicano Worker

The Chicano Worker

by Vernon M. Briggs, Jr., Walter Fogel,
and Fred H. Schmidt

University of Texas Press Austin & London

Library of Congress Cataloging in Publication Data

Briggs, Vernon M
    The Chicano worker.

    Bibliography: p.
    Includes index.
        1. Mexican Americans—Employment—Southwest, New. 2. Mexican
Americans—Employment—United States. I. Fogel, Walter A., joint author.
II. Schmidt, Fred H., joint author. III. Title.
HD8081.M6B74   331.6'3'6872073   76-28237
ISBN 0-292-71040-2

Copyright © 1977 by the University of Texas Press

Printed in the United States of America

Contents

ACKNOWLEDGMENTS ix

INTRODUCTION xi

1. THE PEOPLE 3

2. LABOR SUPPLY 26

3. INCOME AND EARNINGS 43

4. THE JOB MARKET 62

5. THE RURAL ECONOMY 78

6. PUBLIC POLICY NEEDS FOR

 FUTURE ECONOMIC OPPORTUNITY 93

NOTES 105

BIBLIOGRAPHY 117

INDEX 125

Tables

1. Population and Income of the Spanish-Heritage
    Designations Used for the *Census of Population:
    1970*, California and Texas   xii
1.1. Spanish-Surname and Spanish-Language–
    Spanish-Surname Population, Southwestern
    States, 1970   7
1.2. Average Family Size, Southwestern States, 1970   9
1.3. Number of Legal Immigrants from Mexico by Fiscal
    Year   13
2.1. Labor Force of the Southwest, 1970   27
2.2. Labor-Force Participation Rates, Southwestern
    States, 1970   28
2.3. Labor-Force Participation Rates by Age and Sex,
    California and Texas, 1970   31
2.4. Unemployment Rates, Southwestern States, 1960 and
    1970   35
2.5. Unemployment Rates by Age and Sex,
    California and Texas, 1970   37
3.1. Median Family Income by Ethnic Origin of Head,
    United States, 1968   45
3.2. Median Family Income of Selected Population
    Groups, California, 1969   46
3.3. Median Income of Spanish-Surname Families,
    Southwestern States, 1969   47
3.4. Median Income of Spanish-Surname Persons,
    Age 25–64, Southwestern States, 1969   50
3.5. Mean Income of Spanish-Surname Persons in the
    Southwest by Nativity Class, 1969   52
3.6. Median Income of Mexican-Origin and All Males
    by School Years Completed, Age 25 and Up,
    United States, 1971   54
3.7. Median Income of Spanish-Surname Families as a
    Percent of Anglo Income, Southwest, 1959
    and 1969   59
3.8. Median Income of Spanish-Surname Males Relative

to Anglos and Females Relative to All Whites, Southwest, 1959 and 1969   61
4.1. Spanish-Surname, Anglo, and Negro Employment
by Occupation, Southwest, 1970   64
4.2. Ratio of Median Earnings by Occupation: Spanish
Language–Spanish Surname to Anglo and Negro,
1969   66
4.3. Ratio of Average Earnings and Job Indexes by
Occupation, Spanish Surname to Anglo, Males, 1959   73
4.4. Occupational Distributions of Mexican American
Men, Southwest, 1930–1970   76
4.5. Occupational Position Indexes of Mexican American
and Anglo Men, 1930–1970   77

Acknowledgments

It is a pleasure to acknowledge the able research assistance provided for this volume by Kenneth Koford and Anne Stevens. Typing assistance was provided by Geneva Alexander, Charlotte Smith, Maria Otto, and Sophia Behrstock. The original version of this study was prepared for the National Manpower Policy Task Force in Washington, D.C. The authors alone, however, are responsible for the accuracy of the contents.

Introduction

This is a small volume about the labor-market experience in the United States of workers who are of Mexican heritage. The first issue facing anyone writing about these persons is what to call them, since there is no consensus on that matter, even among the Mexican-heritage population. The term chosen for that purpose and used, for the most part, throughout the text is *Chicano*. This choice runs counter to the more traditional use of the appellation *Mexican American* (as used, for example, in the monumental study *The Mexican-American People*).[1] Although the authors do not have strong feelings on the matter, the term *Chicano* rather than *Mexican American* does seem, at this time, to be more closely associated with the rising level of ethnic consciousness and the movement for equitable treatment which is occurring among persons of Mexican origin in the United States. More than anything else, the predominant use of *Chicano* in this volume reflects the authors' concerned support for these events. In order to avoid extreme style redundancy, however, and in recognition of its frequent use, the term *Mexican American* is also used occasionally to refer to the subject population.

A rather more complex matter is the choice of the appropriate statistically defined population so as best to describe workers of Mexican descent. The *Census of Population*, 1970, which necessarily is the source of most of our statistics, presents three alternatives: (1) the Spanish-surname population, as measured exclusively in five southwestern states; (2) the Spanish-language—Spanish-surname population, tabulated only for the same five southwestern states; and (3) the Mexican-origin population, which is enumerated for the entire United States. Largely on the criteria of comparability with earlier statistics and the amount of statistical detail available, the Spanish-surname population was selected and is used wherever possible in this volume to present statistical information. Mexican-origin statistics are used to provide information about Chicano experiences outside the southwestern region and are also used when noncensus

TABLE 1. *Population and income of the Spanish-heritage designations used for the "Census of Population: 1970," California and Texas*

Census designation	California Population	California Median 1969 family income	Texas Population	Texas Median 1969 family income
Spanish language– Spanish surname	3,102,000	$8,791	2,059,671	$5,897
Spanish surname	2,222,000	8,427	1,663,567	5,603
Spanish origin	2,369,000	8,297	1,841,000	5,666
Mexican origin	1,857,000	8,050	1,619,000	5,430

Sources: U.S. Bureau of the Census, *Census: 1970, General Social and Economic Characteristics*, PC(1)-C6,*California*, table 48, p. 385, table 57, p. 403; and PC(1)-C45, *Texas*, table 48, p. 433, table 57, p. 451. Idem, "Persons of Spanish Origin," *Census: 1970, Subject Reports*, PC(2)-1C, table 3, pp. 11, 29, and table 10, pp. 123 and 134; and "Persons of Spanish Surname," PC(2)-1D, table 1, p. 1, table 12, pp. 82 and 83.

sources, for example, the *Current Population Reports*, must be employed.[2]

The Spanish-language–Spanish-surname measure, of course, provides a larger count of persons than does the Spanish-surname concept alone—the former includes Spanish-surname persons plus all other persons in families where the mother tongue of the head or wife was Spanish. A good deal of statistical detail is also available for the Spanish-language–Spanish-surname (SLSS) designation. Its use, however, would have biased comparisons with earlier statistics (it was first utilized for the 1970 *Census of Population*) and would have added an inappropriate component to our subject population. This is best illustrated by the data in table 1.

The median family income of the California SLSS population in 1969 was $364 higher than that of Spanish-surname families in the state. The median family income of the segment of the SLSS population which did not have Spanish surnames was approximately $9,670,[3] or almost 90 percent of the figure for all white families in California. The SLSS designation adds a population component to the Spanish-surname measure which cannot be realistically characterized as disadvantaged—at least in terms of income. Since the major justification for this volume is a hoped-for policy concern with a disadvantaged population, the SLSS concept is less appropriate for our purposes than the Spanish-surname measure.

There may be some tangential value in offering an explanation for the comparatively large income of Spanish-language persons who do not have Spanish surnames. Logically, much of this population segment must consist of people in families where the head is Anglo and the wife is of Spanish origin—families which result from marriages of Chicanas to Anglo men.* (If the mother tongue of the wife—the language that she spoke at home as a child—is Spanish, the entire family is counted as part of the "Spanish-language" population.) Apparently, many Chicanas are "marrying up" in the sense that they marry Anglo men who earn larger incomes than the average Spanish-surname male. This phenomenon is consistent with the general tendency of women to marry up in the American society.

Returning to the census measures, Table 1 indicates that a focus on the disadvantaged would be best served by using the "Mexican-origin" statistics since Mexican-origin families have the lowest incomes of any of the possible statistical groups. Unfortunately, however, the 1970 *Census* was the first to use this self-designation;[4] consequently, comparability with prior years is impossible. About 15 percent of the Spanish-surname population in the Southwest is not of Mexican origin, but intertemporal comparability is possible only for the Spanish-surname population.

To the reader who is now confused by definitional and measurement complexity, the following summary guidelines are offered. (1) *Chicano* is the term primarily used to designate our subject's population; occasionally *Mexican American* is used interchangeably with it. (2) Most of our statistics refer to the Spanish-surname population as measured by the *Census*; however, some use of SLSS and Mexican-origin data was required.

---

* The word *Anglo* is used in the text to indicate the group that remains once the Spanish-surnamed population is subtracted from the "white" category used by the U.S. Bureau of the Census.

(3) For the sake of precision, all statistics will be associated with the *Census* populations from which they were obtained (Spanish surname, Mexican origin, SLSS) rather than with the generic term *Chicano*.

Most of the material in this volume will focus on an area referred to as the Southwest; it consists of five contiguous states—Arizona, California, Colorado, New Mexico, and Texas. Most (87 percent) of the Mexican-origin population of the country lives in these states and, for measurement purposes, the Spanish-surname population is enumerated only in these states. It would, however, be a mistake to think of Chicanos as an ethnic population of only regional concern. Their size is significant (over 6 million), especially when combined with other Spanish-origin persons in the United States (the total exceeded 11 million in 1975), and they are working and living outside the Southwest in increasing numbers. More importantly, policies which are effectively responsive to the needs of this population must be formulated and carried out at the national rather than regional level. The institutions and mechanisms necessary to do the job are simply not available on a regional basis.

Only within the last ten years has there been a national recognition of both the size and the disadvantaged status of the Chicano and other Spanish-heritage populations. In part, this recognition has occurred because the population of these groups, particularly Chicanos, is increasing so rapidly. It remains to be seen whether the current attention will grow or whether it is merely an ephemeral product of opportunistic desires by public officials. Clearly, the multifold problems faced by this ethnic group are not going to disappear. Instead, Chicanos are becoming increasingly aware of the problems they face in their efforts to obtain an equitable share of the benefits of the American society—problems of schooling, housing, health, employment, social status, and cultural identity. It is almost certain that they will become increasingly active in seeking solutions to these problems, through their own efforts and through assistance from the larger society.

One of the greatest needs of Chicanos is improvement in their labor-market experiences—better jobs and incomes. Good jobs with adequate incomes help to provide better schooling, health, and other benefits. This volume is about the Chicano worker, but the material presented here has important implications for other aspects of Chicano life as well.

The first chapter of this book presents background material on the demographic and other characteristics of Chicanos. Chapter 2 deals with Chicano labor supply. The next two chapters go to the core of Chicano labor-market experience with descriptions of their income and job status. Chapter 5 presents a view of the important rural experience of this ethnic group. The final chapter puts much of the previous material into a larger perspective and provides some assessments of present and future needs which are relevant to both private and public policy.

1. The People

Introduction

Historical factors are extremely important to the contemporary understanding of the differential economic status of the major racial groups in American society. For a study of group differences, every school child knows where to begin for blacks and for American Indians. For the former, it is slavery; for the latter, it is the subjugation begun by the Spanish *conquistadores* in the 1500's and completed by the United States military campaigns of the 1860–1890 period which confined the surviving tribes to desolate rural reservations. For Chicanos, however, the proper starting point is seldom acknowledged on the regional level and hardly known at the national level. Yet, the weight of their treatment in history is no less burdensome for Chicanos than the treatment of all other minority groups has been for them.

The settlement of the Southwest was a violent and tumultuous process. The violence of the region long preceded the arrival of the Anglos, but it certainly did not end after their coming. The events leading to the Mexican War of 1846–1848 had their antecedents with the settlement of Anglos in the area that has become part of the state of Texas. Although the original Anglo settlers were invited to move into eastern Texas, conflicts and ill will soon developed as the Anglo population grew and began to exceed the Mexican population. Efforts by Mexico to stop further Anglo settlement were futile. In 1836 Texas successfully revolted from Mexican rule. With the creation of the independent Republic of Texas came a decade of constant turmoil and guerilla warfare. No peace treaty was ever signed. In 1845, Texas was annexed by the United States and the ensuing war with Mexico was virtually inevitable. Fought with large numbers of undisciplined volunteers, the war involved numerous violent atrocities committed by the United States military forces against the Mexican civilian population.[1] Admitting the atrocities, General Winfield Scott later stated that his forces had "committed atrocities to make Heaven weep and every American of Christian morals blush for his country."[2] Aside from the unnecessary violence, the fact that the war was totally imperialistic in nature has made the Mexican War of 1846–1848 a permanent blot upon the military history of the nation.

The war was formally terminated by the Treaty of Guadalupe Hidalgo in 1848. Because the treaty ceded not only land but also people, the Mexican negotiators insisted that extensive protections be given to guarantee both the property and the civil rights of their former citizens. Thus, as Carey McWilliams has pointedly observed, "It should never be forgotten that, with the exception of the Indians, Mexicans are the only minority in the United States who were annexed by conquest; the only minority, Indians again excepted, whose rights were specifically safeguarded by treaty provision."[3]

The Mexican War had been fought over the control of land—not people. When the war ended, the last large area of land to be added to the United States by conquest was accomplished. The area was approximately one-half of all the land that Mexico possessed at the time. But the changes for the people of the region did not cease with the peace treaty. For despite the treaty guarantees, the protections of previous landownership rights were soon scuttled by a combination of legal ambiguity, purposeful trickery, and outright violence. How much of each is debatable but the outcome is not. The people of Mexican heritage who once shared control of the land with the Indians quickly became a minority people who were dependent upon the Anglo landowners for their employment and income opportunities.

Thus, although the ancestors of the present-day Chicano population were not formally enslaved as were blacks, they did carry the stigma of having fought and been conquered in battle with the United States. A stamp of social inferiority was imposed throughout the Southwest that, operationally, was quite similar to a system of overt segregation. It was not as rigid as that placed upon blacks in the Southeast but it did have many social, psychological, political, and economic similarities with respect to its lasting impacts. As McWilliams has succinctly written, "The notion that Mexicans are interlopers who are never to be counted in any reckoning dies but slowly in the Southwest."[4] It was in this subservient relationship that the waves of immigrants from Mexico in the twentieth century (from whom the vast

majority of the present-day Chicano population are the descend-
ants) found themselves upon their arrival.

Population

Over nine million persons in the United States reported themselves as being of Spanish origin in the 1970 census. Over one-
half of them were of Mexican origin, and just over a majority of
these were either first- or second-generation immigrants from
Mexico, either having been born there or having had one or
both parents born in that country.[5] As stated in the Introduction, the statistical focus of this volume is largely on the
Spanish-surname population of the Southwest. Table 1.1 presents population figures for that region and its component states.
For comparison purposes, figures for the Spanish-language–
Spanish-surname definition are included as well as those for just
the Spanish-surname population. By either measurement concept, Chicanos are the largest minority in the population of each
of the southwestern states.

Not only are the Spanish surnamed the largest minority in the
Southwest, but their numbers are increasing at a rate which is
much more rapid than is the case for the general population or
for Negroes. Definitive statements about the rate of population
growth of Chicanos are impossible to make because of the definitional and "undercount" problems which have plagued the count
of this group in the decennial censuses of population (more on
this below). The published figures for the Spanish-surname
population of the Southwest show an increase of 54 percent from
1950 to 1960 and 33 percent from 1960 to 1970. The decline in
rate of growth between the two decades (assuming accuracy of
the *Census* figures) is substantially less than for other United
States population groups.

Despite the visibility of Chicanos wherever they are located,
it is apparent that their total number was underenumerated by
the *Census*. The U.S. Bureau of the Census has announced that
it missed about 5.3 million persons in the 1970 count and ac-
knowledges that in doing so it missed counting 7.7 percent of the
black population, largely in inner city areas.[6] It is not known
how many Chicanos were missed; however, it is not improbable

that the percentage would be even higher than it was for blacks. The *Census* enumeration was based on an English-only questionnaire except for areas known to contain large Spanish-speaking populations. The fact that almost one-half of Spanish-surnamed adults had not gone beyond the eighth grade, and that Spanish was the primary language of so many, suggests a large possibility for error. Add to this the problems of bilingual illiteracy, the inability of most census enumerators to converse in Spanish, the understandable fear illegal aliens have of any governmental representative, the extended family relationships and the large number of Chicanos in agriculture who are still migratory workers, and it is clear why the total of those missed is unlikely to ever become known.[7]

The Population Commission of California, a private organization composed of representatives of various Chicano organizations, is one of the groups that has brought suit against the Bureau of the Census seeking some acknowledgment of the scope of the undercount. The commission contends that, in April 1973, about 17.5 percent, or 3.75 million, of the persons in California were Spanish surnamed, with more than 95 percent of these of Mexican descent. (The 1970 *Census* reported only 2.2 million Spanish-surname persons.) The commission predicts that, by 1980, Spanish-surnamed residents will be one-fourth of the population of Los Angeles County. Already there are more persons of Mexican descent in Los Angeles than in any city other than Mexico City itself.

After this volume was nearly completed, the U.S. Bureau of the Census revised its estimate of the Spanish-origin population in the United States to 10.6 million in 1973 from 9.2 million in 1970. The 1973 figure is 16 percent larger than the 1970 *Census* count of 9.1 million. The 1973 estimate of the Mexican-origin population is 6.3 million compared to 4.5 million in 1970—an increase of almost 40 percent! The new estimates obviously mean that the populations and percentages in table 1.1 err on the low side, but by how much is not possible to say since the 1973 data are not reported by state or region. Although the Bureau of the Census believes that, "all told, population growth [natural increase plus immigration] for the period from April 1970 to March 1973 may account for close to two-thirds of the difference between the 1970 census and the March 1973 figures," this is largely speculation because estimates of the

TABLE 1.1. *Spanish-surname and Spanish-language–Spanish-surname population, southwestern states, 1970*

(In thousands)

	Total population	Spanish surname		SLSS*	
		number	% total	number	% total
Southwest	36,147	4,668	12.9	6,188	17.1
Arizona	1,771	246	13.9	333	18.8
California	19,957	2,222	11.1	3,102	15.5
Colorado	2,207	212	9.6	286	13.0
New Mexico	1,016	324	31.9	407	40.1
Texas	11,195	1,663	14.9	2,060	18.4

Sources: U.S. Bureau of the Census, "Persons of Spanish Origin," *Census: 1970, Subject Reports*, PC(2)-1C, table 1, pp. 1–6, table 10, pp. 121–134; and "Persons of Spanish Surname," PC(2)-1D, table 1, pp. 1–2, table 12, pp. 81–83. Idem, *Census: 1970, General Social and Economic Characteristics*, PC(1)-C6, *California*, table 49, pp. 387–388, table 57, pp. 403–404; and PC(1)-C45, *Texas*, table 49, pp. 435–436, table 57, pp. 451–452.

*Spanish language–Spanish surname.

separate effects of the bureau's own changes in methods, origin identifications, and sample size and design have not been made. In view of its rapid increase, high priority should be given by government and private demographers to analysis of the recent growth of the Mexican-origin population.[8]

Birth Rates of a Growing Minority

Chicanas comprise one of the most fertile groups in the population of the United States. The fertility of women of Mexican origin presently has the potential of doubling their number in a single generation, whereas the rate for all white women implies an increase of only 40 percent per generation. The national replacement quota for all women 35 to 44 years old is 2,070 children per 1,000 women, but Mexican-origin women of that age group in recent years have greatly exceeded that figure by having 4,429 children per 1,000 women. Furthermore, among women of Mexican origin, the number who are 15 to 24 years of age is much greater than the number who are 25 to 34 years of age. The difference exceeds that which prevails among other ethnic groups, according to a survey of fertility variations made by the Bureau of the Census.[9] This predominance of younger females suggests that the present high rate of population increase among persons of Mexican origin is likely to continue into the future. Spanish-surnamed persons have a median age of only 20.2 years, a figure that is much below that of the total population and even less than that for Negroes.[10]

A high birthrate is one of the factors which makes families and households of Chicanos larger than is the case for the population as a whole. Table 1.2 shows how these families compare in size to all families in the 1970 *Census*—generally about one-fourth larger. However, it is important to note that the average size of Spanish-surnamed families decreased at a greater rate from 1960 to 1970 than did families in the total population.

The increase in the Chicano population through birth would be enough in itself to ensure that there will be a growing awareness of this group, not just in the Southwest, but throughout the nation. Two other trends make this national awareness even more likely. One is the continuing large increments to the Chicano population through immigration, making Chicanos the most rapidly growing minority in the country, and the other is their migration out of and through the Southwest to other parts of the nation.

Persons of Mexican origin tend to concentrate according to their historical patterns of original residence or settlement as immigrants to the United States. This makes them a steadily growing component of the population in the Southwest. A similar tendency has made Puerto Ricans a substantial segment in the populations of New York and New Jersey and has also made Cubans a large part of the population of Florida.

Although persons acknowledging Mexican origin are but one of the components in the Chicano population, they are over-

TABLE 1.2. *Average family size, southwestern states, 1970*

| | All families | | Spanish-surname families | |
	1960	1970	1960	1970
Arizona	3.82	3.65	4.87	4.54
California	3.51	3.47	4.29	4.20
Colorado	3.62	3.54	4.69	4.29
New Mexico	4.03	3.85	4.73	4.32
Texas	3.72	3.59	5.03	4.67

Sources: U.S. Bureau of the Census, "Persons of Spanish Surname," *Census: 1970, Subject Reports*, PC(2)-1D, table 11, pp. 78–80. Idem, "Persons of Spanish Surname," *Census: 1960, Subject Reports*, PC(2)-1B, table 5, pp. 36–37. Idem, *Census: 1970, Detailed Characteristics*, PC(1)-D1, *U.S. Summary*, table 333, p. 1628. Idem, *Census: 1960*, vol. 1, *Characteristics of the Population*, pt. 1, *U.S. Summary*, table 280, p. 759.

whelmingly the largest one in most southwestern states. Many of the Spanish-surnamed inhabitants of the region have familial ties with Mexico that go back so many generations that they no longer acknowledge origins stemming from that country; others come from families that trace their beginning in this country to a time when Santa Fe was a provincial capital for Spain—years before the English founded Jamestown on the eastern seaboard. Others, of course, have origins in countries other than Mexico—in Central America or South America. Persons acknowledging Mexican origin in the five states range from 4.7 percent of the total population in Colorado to 14.4 percent in Texas.[11] However, persons spoken of here as Chicano or Mexican American represent substantially higher percentages of the population of these states—11.9 percent in Colorado and 16.4 percent in Texas. In New Mexico persons who acknowledge a national origin in Mexico constitute only 11.7 percent of the population, but when the census identifier of Spanish surname is applied it is found that 31.9 percent of that state's population has such names. Most of these people have roots that are buried

deep in the land of that state, from a time before there was a
Mexico. "They have always lived in the same area, only the
ownership and the name has changed," which is why the de-
scendants of the original settlers of New Mexico and California
often prefer to be identified as Hispanos and Californios.[12]

Although the migration of persons of Mexican origin to states
outside the Southwest is substantial in number, only in Illinois,
Kansas, Nevada, Utah, and Idaho has it been of sufficient scope
to enable Mexican Americans to account for more than 1 percent
of any state's population outside the Southwest. Nonetheless, in
Michigan, Indiana, Ohio, Wisconsin, New York, Florida, and
Washington there are substantial numbers of persons of Mexican
origin—more than in any of the aforementioned states, except
Illinois and Kansas. There are more persons of Mexican origin in
Illinois than in either Colorado or New Mexico, but they represent only 1.5 percent of that state's population. However, here
again, when the *Census* identifier of Spanish origin is applied to
the 1970 Illinois population, this percentage rises to 3.5, or
390,000 persons, a number sufficient to make the Spanish-origin
population of considerable significance as a minority group in
that state and highly visible in the metropolitan areas in which
they are located.

Immigration

Chicanos are the only ethnic group in the U.S. population that
still receives large increases in its total number through a cease-
less stream of immigrants, most of whom enter illegally. Mexico
is the source of most of this increase. Two aspects of this situation are crucial to an understanding of how this comes about and
why it is a situation that does not lend itself to any easy control.
One is the physical nature of the border, which runs for over
1,800 miles between the two countries.

Starting at the Gulf of Mexico, the border begins as a natural
boundary in the form of the Rio Grande. However, this is an
uncertain river in many of its stretches at various times. It
meanders when in flood stage, cutting off a loop of land to put
Mexican real estate on the U.S. side, or taking U.S. territory
and putting it on the Mexican side; it dips underground in places
to run invisibly under the sand. In drought years it sometimes

just gets tired of running at all. It is a river, according to a Texas brag, that can be plowed. Certainly, there are points where it can be waded. This tenuous natural boundary extends only to El Paso, the historic passage to the north used by the *conquistadores*. From El Paso west there are no natural features to the boundary as it runs up steep mountains and down deep barrancas and across unmarked desert areas. In recent years the United States has begun to fence portions of the boundary that invite the unchecked passage of people across the border. There are not too many such places, however, for this is a forbidding area in most of its length. The towns along the border are oasis communities in two parts—one part on the Mexican side, the other on the U.S. side. Each of these twin communities maintains a symbiotic relationship between its two parts, in the dependency and traffic between its people and in the economies of their respective communities.

The other central fact about this border is that no other border in the world separates two nations having as great a disparity in the per capita personal incomes of their people as exists between the average citizen of the United States and Mexico. Per capita incomes in 1971 were $5,350 and $720, respectively. The difference exceeds the per capita income of any other nation in the world except Sweden. Thus, whereas Canada has a per capita personal income that compares favorably with the United States, this is nowhere near the case in Mexico. The income difference is an enormous economic incentive for many Mexicans to move northward as a means of improving their prospects for jobs and income. Many ingenious ways have been contrived for them to do so.

The border between the two countries was for all practical purposes an open one until 1924, when the Immigration and Naturalization Act of that year was passed and the Border Patrol created. Prior to 1924, and in practice for a number of years thereafter, Mexican workers were welcomed to this country for unskilled work, just as were the Irish, Poles, southern Europeans, and others, until the gates of immigration were all but closed. The 1924 act established quotas for immigration from Eastern Hemisphere nations and unlimited immigration, in theory, for those in the Western Hemisphere. In the decade of the 1920's, over .5 million legal immigrants came from Mexico. Also, that decade saw the start of the "commuter" arrangement whereby Mexican nationals received immigration visas permitting them to work in the United States as fictional residents of this country while actually continuing to reside across the border in Mexico. This legal fiction continues today.

During the depression decade of the 1930's, immigration from Mexico declined to a trickle, and the traffic flowed the other way as several hundred thousand persons were repatriated to Mexico. Mexicans were not welcome during that bleak period in the competition for jobs or as participants in the relief programs instituted during the decade. The flow of *legal* immigrants from Mexico is shown in table 1.3. In the 1940's, only about 60,000 Mexican immigrants came into the United States, but a contract labor program was started in that decade as a means of bringing Mexican workers into agriculture during the wartime period of labor shortages. This "bracero program" became formalized by legislation and persisted for twenty-two years after its start in 1942. (The program is discussed more extensively in chapter 5.) Almost .5 million workers a year would enter for short periods of work, and many who could not get into this program and sought escape from the unemployment prevalent in Mexico entered the country illegally. Over 800,000 illegally entered Mexicans were apprehended in the 1940's. But this was only the beginning of the large-scale surreptitious entries which have continued up to the present.[13]

During the 1950's, only 300,000 legal immigrants entered the United States from Mexico, but about 3 million contract workers were brought in for short periods under the bracero program. In that decade the so-called wetback flood was running at full tide. The Border Patrol apprehended over 3.4 million Mexican aliens and returned them to Mexico. There is, of course, no way to determine how many undocumented persons went unapprehended.

The Immigration and Nationality Act of 1952 changed the immigration policies of the United States to specify that the first half of the immigration quotas allocated should be filled by persons possessing high skills, and the remaining half by their close relatives. Even so, in the 1960's there were 443,000 legal immigrants from Mexico and over 1.5 million braceros, while the number of illegal immigrants apprehended was 770,000.

Declarations made by Mexican immigrants as to their intended permanent residence provide some clues about favored

TABLE 1.3. *Number of legal immigrants from Mexico by fiscal year*

1950—6,740	1941–1950—60,590
1960—32,680	1951–1960—299,810
1970—44,820	1961–1970—543,940
1971—50,320	1971–1975—318,461
1972—64,210	
1973—70,140	
1974—71,586	
1975—62,205	

Sources: U.S. Bureau of the Census, "Persons of Spanish Surname," *Census: 1970, Subject Reports*, PC(2)-1D, table 1, pp. 1–6. Idem, *Census: 1970, Number of Inhabitants*, PC(1)-A1, *U.S. Summary*, table 8, pp. 48–49. Idem, *Census: 1970, General Social and Economic Characteristics*, PC(1)-C4, *Arizona*, table 49, pp. 93–94; PC(1)-C6, *California*, table 49, pp. 387–388; PC(1)-C7, *Colorado*, table 49, pp. 142–143; PC(1)-C33; *New Mexico*, table 49, pp. 100–101; and PC(1)-C45, *Texas*, table 49, pp. 435–436.

locations. In 1970, over one-half of the 44,400 legal immigrants stated an intention to reside in California. A little over 13,000 preferred residence in Texas, while Illinois was third among their preferences, with over 3,000 declaring they would settle in that state. The remaining location choices were distributed among New Mexico, Michigan, New York, Washington, and Colorado.[14]

The distributions by age and sex suggest that legal Mexican immigrants generally came in family groups equally divided between males and females. In the fiscal year ending in June 1971, over one-half of the 50,100 immigrants were under 20 years of age, while only 3 percent were over 60 years of age, and 45 percent were between the ages of 20 and 60. This contrasts sharply with persons immigrating under the Cuban Refugee Program, for example, who are generally older, with a little over a quarter of their number under 20 years of age, 13 percent over 60 years of age, and females significantly outnumbering males.[15]

Even among the legal immigrants from Mexico, the vast majority of those who are workers are from unskilled or menial occupations. In 1971 there were 50,000 Mexican immigrants admitted, 34,800 of whom were dependents. Of the 15,300 who were family heads, almost 80 percent had occupations as laborers, private household workers, or service workers, and less than 10 percent were white-collar workers. Less than 4 percent were classified as professional or technical workers.[16]

The figures on legal immigration do not take the full measure of the worker traffic across the border. The number of persons who enjoyed "commuter" status rose considerably between 1960 and 1970, and this became a major component of the labor supply in the U.S. counties adjacent to the border (see chapter 5). Estimates of the current number of commuters range from 60,000 to 100,000 per day.

Border Crossers and Illegal Immigrants

There is yet another category of persons in the labor supply of the Southwest: the border crossers, who have permits to enter this country for seventy-two hours for visiting, business, or pleasure. Their permits are not for work, but in fact are widely used for such purpose, since there is no effective way to determine where these persons go or what they do once entry has been gained. If they are caught working, their cards are taken from them. Given a job, they are, of course, docile employees, easily victimized in the job market, as are all undocumented aliens.

Finally, there are those who enter with truly fraudulent papers. The forging of documents and the purchase of illicit passage and transportation are a big business in the Southwest. The

underground railroad that whisked southern slaves to freedom
prior to the Civil War was an amateurish effort compared to the
professional expertise applied to bringing Mexican workers into
the country. It is a profitable trade for those engaged in it.[17]

Early in 1973 federal authorities seized 60,000 counterfeit
alien registration cards (Forms I-151) and engraving plates in a
bus station in Los Angeles, stating, "They were so perfectly
done that they would sell for $500 each in Mexico."[18] Immigra-
tion officials themselves have spoken out on their inability to
control the situation and have called present immigration con-
trols a "nearly complete failure."[19] They add that at the border
checkpoint San Ysidro 2,333 counterfeit entry documents were
detected in 1972, which they felt represented less than 10 percent of the illegal documents used by immigrants arriving at that
station in 1972. Estimates of the number of illegal aliens arriving
annually in the Los Angeles area alone have been placed at from
300,000 to 500,000, or more, by immigration officials, who add,
"You would need a crystal ball to tell."[20] Their efforts to control
the situation have been complicated by recent disclosures of
corruption among Immigration and Naturalization Service (INS)
agents. Several immigration officials have been indicted for dealing in fraudulent documents.[21]

Illegal entry into the United States is a misdemeanor for a first
offense and a felony thereafter. However, as a matter of practice
aliens are not prosecuted unless they have a criminal record or a
long list of illegal entries. Instead, they are returned to Mexico.
The records of formal deportations year by year do not reflect
the number of these refugees, since most apprehended persons
readily agree to being returned to Mexico without warrant procedures.

The large INS task force that began predawn raids on barrio
hotels, apartment buildings, and factories in Los Angeles in June
1973 hired independent bus drivers to ferry those apprehended
to border points. The avowed purpose of the raids was to ap-
prehend a total of 100,000 aliens by the end of the year. The task
force had exceeded their first month's quota by 1,500 when a
court order stopped the operation. An injunction was obtained
after the American Civil Liberties Union brought a class action
suit against INS, charging that hapless U.S. citizens were being
picked up in schools, homes, and offices and transported out of

the country. But the border aliens themselves submitted cheer-
fully to the process, knowing that they could be back in Los
Angeles in a few hours or days. One bitter deportation officer
was quoted in the press, "They should either give us the tools
we need to get rid of the aliens or admit that we want them in
the U.S. as slave labor."[22]

Throughout the Southwest the recurring news stories about
the apprehension of Mexican nationals at their places of work
receive a "ho-hum" response by all except those most directly
affected. Only when these raids are brought to national attention
is there any but local awareness that this problem exists (as when
Mrs. Ramona Bañuelos was before the Senate Finance Committee for confirmation as treasurer of the United States and insisted that she knew nothing about the employment of illegal
aliens in her California business, although there had been six
previous raids by the INS to remove aliens from the plant).[23]

The repetitiousness of news accounts about the apprehension
of Mexicans unlawfully working in this country is but a reminder
that the Border Patrol, understaffed as it is, can on occasion
exert itself to stir the surface of this labor pool but is generally
unable to stem its growth. Its size is unknown, but it does constitute a shadow labor force in the Southwest. Thus, the official
governmental figures on immigration from Mexico provide
only one dimension of a labor supply that has at least two other
hidden dimensions.

Since we are a country which does not resort to centrally
issued work permits, where citizenship is not applied as a test to
one's right to work, and where it is not difficult to get one or
more Social Security cards, there is no way to provide more
rigorous surveillance over Mexican nationals working in the
United States without harassment to Mexican American citizens. Whereas blue-eyed, blond-headed persons may be readily
waved through a border checkpoint, most Chicanos will be
stopped. A Border Patrol sweep of an industrial plant can impose on all Chicano citizens the burden of proving that they are
not strangers in their own land. Anyone who has ever been
detained even momentarily as a suspect where some offense has
been committed knows the discomfort and quiet rage this can
engender. Many Chicano citizens must contend with this as a
recurring intrusion upon their freedom. It is understandable
that some Chicanos oppose proposed legislation that would

bring sanctions against employers for knowingly hiring illegal aliens. This could require all Chicanos to meet a test that most workers need never confront.

Mobility in the United States

There is evidence from the 1970 *Census* that new migration patterns are developing for Chicanos within the United States. Although California and Texas appear to have been the pre-ferred places of residence for immigrants from Mexico in recent years, there is clear indication that a growing number are mov-ing, along with other Spanish-origin persons, to other states in the West.

That portion of the Spanish-surname population which is foreign born has been declining in the last two decades in each of the southwestern states except California. Colorado and New Mexico received only negligible immigration from Mexico in the last decade. But in six other western states—Idaho, Iowa, Kan-sas, Nebraska, Oregon, and Washington—over 10 percent of the Spanish-origin population is foreign born.[24] Furthermore, in these states the percentage of the Spanish-origin population born within the state of residence is in every case less than is true for any of the southwestern states. This would indicate a movement of native-born and immigrant Chicanos to these new locations.[25]

Much of the migration into Washington and Oregon has come from Texas and California. Relatively few Chicanos have moved into the sparsely populated Rocky Mountain states, and most of those who have done so came from the nearby states of Colorado and New Mexico. The midwestern area, especially Chicago, seems to have gained a considerable number of Mexican Ameri-cans, largely from Texas, but also from farther west and from the Great Lakes area. Only 44 and 52 percent, respectively, of the Mexican-origin persons living in Illinois and Michigan in 1970, the two midwestern states with the largest numbers of Mexican Americans, were born in their state of residence. Almost one-third of the Illinois Chicanos were foreign born, presumably in Mexico.

The characteristics of these migrants show them to be rela-tively young and well educated. In some of the states they have education and income levels equivalent to that of the state's population as a whole. It can be conjectured that the movement of Chicanos to the northern areas of the West is composed in substantial part of a younger, more upwardly mobile generation comprising those who are leaving areas of little opportunity and high discrimination for a region of greater opportunity.

Part of the migratory shifting of Mexican Americans from place to place has apparently come about as part of the movement of people from rural to urban areas. This movement has been more pronounced for Chicanos than for Anglos. In the 1950 and 1960 censuses, Anglos in the Southwest were more urbanized than Chicanos. However, at the time of the 1970 *Census*, Chicanos overtook Anglos in the extent of their urbanization. In each of the five states except New Mexico, a higher percentage of Chicanos lived in urban areas than did Anglos.

It seems reasonable to speculate that the major factors accounting for the relatively high degree of urbanization of Chicanos lie in a very limited amount of farm ownership or tenancy, the declining work opportunities in agriculture, and the fact that more of the Anglo than Chicano nonurban population in the Southwest consists of rural nonfarm families who have incomes which are independent of the rural economy. Furthermore, a very high proportion of those Chicanos who have some dependency on agricultural employment do not live in rural areas. Many barrios or *colonias* which house Chicano farm laborers have, since World War II, been encompassed by urban sprawl, whereas formerly they were satellite communities classified as rural.

Two other trends are detectable in the migration of Chicanos: the ascendancy of California as the El Dorado for Chicanos in the Southwest and their movement away from the border counties in the Southwest. At the time of the 1960 *Census*, Texas and California each accounted for about 41 percent of the region's Chicano residents. By 1970 California accounted for one-half of this population and Texas accounted for only one-third; the proportions in the other three states did not change appreciably. Over 40 percent of the California Chicano population was born in a foreign country or another state. The increase in Spanish-surname persons in California represented a startling 53 percent growth within the census period.

In 1960, 19 percent of the region's Chicano population resided in the tier of twenty-five U.S. counties immediately adjacent to the border of Mexico. By 1970 this percentage had dropped to 16, although those counties retained the same 8 percent proportion of the region's total population from 1960 to 1970. One of the cities that became a principal recipient of this Chicano migration was Houston (presumably because of its rapid economic growth), which in 1960 ranked tenth in an array of metropolitan areas having the largest number of Chicanos. By 1970, Houston was in fourth place. The complete array for 1970 placed Los Angeles at the head of the list with 1,289,000 Chicanos (Spanish-language–Spanish-surname persons). San Antonio was second with less than a third of that number, 385,000. San Francisco–Oakland placed a close third with 363,900, and Houston was next with 212,000, followed by El Paso; San Bernardino–Riverside Counties, San Jose, San Diego, and Orange County, California; and Hidalgo County, Texas. The last two had not even been in the list of the top ten in 1960.[26] (Use of the Mexican-origin definition places Chicago on the list, following El Paso.)

Educational Disadvantages

One would have had to experience it himself or have been a sensitive student-observer to comprehend readily the educational deprivation which has been experienced by most Chicano workers in the Southwest, a deprivation that continues today for most of their children. This loss of educational opportunity in generations past casts long shadows into the future, committing many Chicanos to working out their lives within those shadows.

The forms of this deprivation are not easily detailed. The U.S. Commission on Civil Rights has produced three volumes to explain to the nation both the crassness of this deprivation and the subtlety of its effects.[27] The schools throughout most of the region have reflected and reinforced a caste system prevailing in the larger community. The dominant Anglo majority in the Southwest has harbored a caste consciousness that assigns inferior status to Mexican Americans. This relegation to inferior status was impressed on students, intentionally or otherwise, by

the school in ways that are now carefully documented, but which
for generations went unchallenged. Ethnic isolation, both by
district and by school, was and is the rule, not the exception.
Part of the perceived mission of the public schools in the Southwest has been, at worst, a demeaning and uprooting—for the
sake of "Americanizing"—of the language and culture of
Chicanos and, at best, an ignoring of their cultural differences as
though they were of no consequence.

The U.S. Commission on Civil Rights concluded that minority
students in the Southwest do not obtain the benefits of public
education at a rate equal to that of their Anglo classmates:
"Without exception, minority students achieve at a lower rate
than Anglos: their school holding power is lower; their reading
achievement is poorer; their repetition of grades is more frequent; their over-ageness is more prevalent; and they participate in extracurricular activities to a lesser degree than their
Anglo counterparts."[28]

The Mexican American Study Project found that in 1960 there
was a difference of 5 years in the median years of school completed by Spanish-surname and Anglo persons age 25 and over.
In 1950 this difference had been 6 years, but in 1960 the median
years completed by the Spanish surnames were 7.1, compared
to 12.1 for Anglos and 9.0 for nonwhites.[29] Differences among
the states in this education gap were considerable. In California
the gap was 3.6 years, but in Texas it was 6.7 years. By 1970,
these gaps had been closed appreciably but still remained dis-
tressingly large. The schooling gap between Anglos and
Chicanos continued to be the smallest in California, at 2.1 years,
and the largest in Texas, at 5.6 years.[30]

The hope that the failures of the past are being corrected in
the present is not altogether warranted. When the educational
attainment of younger Chicanos vis à vis younger Anglos is
examined, a dismal picture emerges. Looking only at persons 18
to 24 years of age, the 1970 Census shows that the percentage of
Anglos having four years of high school or some college ranges
from 66 in Texas to 74 in California and Colorado; for Chicanos
the range is from 40 percent in Texas to 56 percent in California.
In each of the five states the educational attainment for Negroes
is substantially higher than it is for Mexican Americans. The
disparity in college graduates between Anglos and Chicanos of
this age group is even more marked. Among Anglos the range is

from 7.4 percent in California and Arizona to 8.7 percent in New Mexico. For Chicanos the percentages who have had four years of college range from a mere 1.6 percent in Arizona to 2.0 in California and Colorado.[31]

The dismal picture on enrollment in higher education shows that, next to American Indians, Chicanos have the greatest degree of underrepresentation among minority groups. Only 1.0 percent of their total population is enrolled, compared to 2.0 percent for blacks and 1.3 percent for Puerto Ricans.[32] And this representation is disproportionately concentrated in the early undergraduate years because of recent efforts to increase minority freshman enrollments and the lower academic survival rates of these minority students.

Interestingly, a U.S. Department of Labor national survey found that among "Spanish-descent" males, the labor-force participation rates for high school graduates were about the same as those for dropouts, whereas for all whites and Negroes, male dropouts had significantly lower labor-force rates than graduates.

One of every three youths of Spanish descent, aged 16 to 24, was a dropout in this survey. Unemployment rates were no different than those for all white dropouts. A profound difference, however, showed up in the occupations entered by graduates and dropouts: 45.2 percent of the Spanish-descent graduates went into white-collar occupations, while only 7.7 percent of the dropouts did so. Anne M. Young, who described the findings from this survey, attributed the high dropout rate of Spanish youth to the limited educational opportunities which had been available to recent Mexican and Puerto Rican immigrants in their native countries, the need to leave school at an early age to support themselves and other family members, and the language barrier that inhibits school attendance.[33]

The U.S. Commission on Civil Rights found that schools in the Southwest use a variety of exclusionary practices that deny Chicano students the use of their language, a pride in their heritage, and the support of their community—thus making it difficult for them to participate fully in the educational process.[34] The commission examined three of the principal programs advanced by educators to deal with this problem: remedial reading, English as a second language, and bilingual education. Only the last requires a modification of the traditional school curriculum, but this modification results, according to the commission, in the most effective program of the three for utilizing both the bilingual and the bicultural aspects of the children involved. However, the commission found at the time of its 1972 report that only 6.5 percent of the Southwest's schools had bilingual programs and that these reached only 2.7 percent of the Chicano student population—about one student out of forty. Those students being instructed in English as a second language were about twice this number, while only a little over a tenth of the region's Chicano students were enrolled in remedial reading courses. Federal funds have been the chief stimulus for inducing schools to adopt bilingual education programs, but states are beginning to respond on their own. California in late 1972 adopted its first statewide program, one that educators say will have to be enriched tenfold to reach all of the .5 million children in the state with a dominant language other than English.[35]

The significance of this development can be assessed from the fact that a Bureau of the Census survey found that Spanish was the principal language spoken in the homes of over 2.6 million persons in the Southwest, and that 70 percent of these persons were native born, not foreign born.[36] However, the same survey made the encouraging disclosure that for persons over 14 years of age the ability to read and write English was inversely related to their age; less than one-half of Chicanos over 45 had this ability, but 95 percent of those in the 14-to-15-year age group could read and write English.[37]

Cultural Differences

In addition to the more measurable factors, there is also the issue of racial and cultural differences as a causal factor for prevailing employment and income differentials between Chicanos and Anglos. Until the 1960's, the importance of these features had been largely neglected by labor economists and public policy makers. With the rise of the civil rights movement and its stress on the significance of race as a predictor of economic welfare in a race-conscious society, these topics have come into vogue. Moreover, as Chicanos have now established large enclaves in Illinois, Michigan, Nebraska, Kansas, and Ohio, the importance of learning who these people are, in a cultural sense, is no longer purely a regional matter of concern.

Anthropologists estimate that 95 percent of Mexican Americans are part Indian and over 40 percent are full-blooded Indians.[38] Although one may question the implied preciseness of these figures, the order of magnitude is not in doubt. Relatively few Spaniards ever came to the New World. Spanish colonization of the Americas was prompted by a desire for conquest and, accordingly, it was imposed upon the indigenous Indian population from above.[39] Recognition of Chicanos at the national level as a distinctly separate racial group within the United States has come only during the past decade.

As to ethnic differences, the most obvious feature of Chicanos is the pervasive retention of the Spanish language. The fact that, unlike other immigrant groups, Chicanos lived in the region before there was a United States, plus the lasting proximity of the Mexican border with its continual cross flows of travelers, visitors, and new immigrants, has meant that Mexican cultural characteristics have been constantly nourished and sustained.

The existence and the significance, if any, of culture as a factor for involuntary discriminatory treatment or of voluntary differences in labor-market participation and activities have been persistent topics of scholarly inquiry. However, Paul Bullock has critically observed that "economists have rarely focused upon the relationship of cultural values to employment patterns."[40] Bullock, in his study of Chicano labor-market experience, found that the cultural values of Chicanos "have been strongly influenced by a folk or rural culture in which organized and continuous striving for future monetary gains plays little part."[41] Bullock contends that this pattern of living—particularly among the poor—promotes a mixture of individualism and family unity which leaves little room for an interest in the broader community. The welfare of the family is stressed with the concurrent duty of youngsters to support the family, even if it means leaving school. Less interest is shown for involvement in societal institutions. The long history of discrimination against Chicanos coupled with the antagonism toward Mexican culture expressed by Anglos has only served to heighten the cultural alienation felt by many Chicanos. Bullock also notes the existence of male dominance of the family, which places an emphasis upon physical occupations as opposed to intellectual endeavors. Women in Chicano families are often discouraged from competing in occupations that can be identified as being male oriented. Bullock does find, however, that there are signs of changes occurring in the roles of Chicanas.

In a similar way, Henry M. Ramírez, formerly the chairman of the President's Committee on Opportunities for Spanish Speaking People, listed in 1972 several cultural differences that he felt applied to Chicanos. They were:

1. The belief that relationships between individuals are more important than competitive, materialistic, or achievement norms
2. Strong family ties
3. "Machismo," meaning male dominance, patriarchy, and emphasis on masculinity
4. A sense of solidarity and pride in a unique heritage
5. Aspirations for professional rather than business or managerial occupations[42]

Indeed, a vast literature that has accumulated over the years indicates the existence of cultural differences and suggests, inferentially, that these differences exert significant influence on labor-market conduct. Examining this precise issue, the comprehensive UCLA Mexican American Study Project completed in 1970 had as one of its most important findings the fact that the cultural distinctiveness of Chicanos is receding rapidly.[43] If true, the implication would be that ethnic differences are diminishing as a possible cause of adverse employment experience. The project dismissed the vast repository of traditional wisdom, which contended that cultural differences do exist, by claiming that most of these studies were conducted in isolated settings or were badly out of date. In place of these findings, research conducted by the project led to the important conclusion that these differences are diminishing. The finding was based on a questionnaire administered in Los Angeles, California, and San Antonio, Texas, both of which have large Mexican American populations. Unfortunately, however, the questionnaire was administered *only* to Chicanos. Hence, what was actually tested was not whether cultural differences exist between Anglos and Chicanos, but, rather, the notions possessed by some researchers of what attitudes Chicanos may have toward a list of

stereotyped cultural impressions. Since the responses of the
Chicano respondents were similar to those of the researchers,
the conclusion was drawn that there is little cultural distinctiveness.[44] The conclusion may be valid but the methodology used
to reach it is hardly convincing. Thus the "cultural differences"
issue remains open. In fact, even the project itself hedged its
own bet when it made the summary judgment that "our analysis
makes it clear that ethnic culture *perhaps more than any other
area* warrants continuing intensive research."[45]

Chicanos, for all their cultural cohesiveness as a people and
persistence in sustaining their culture, have been less forceful
and articulate than blacks in seeking redress of their announced
grievances against the larger society. Their cultural differences,
such as that of language, often seem to diminish their ability to
participate in the processes by which changes are accomplished.
For instance, English literacy requirements, education, low
naturalization rates, and the uncertain citizenship status of many
Chicanos effectively reduce their participation in political elections. This is measurable from their voter registration rates
compared to other groups. In 1972 only 44.4 percent of persons
of Spanish origin who were of voting age were registered to vote.
Comparable figures for Negroes and Anglos were 65.5 and 73.4
percent respectively.[46]

2. Labor Supply

A very substantial part of the supply of labor in the economy of the Southwest comes from the rapidly growing Chicano population. Chicanos are a significant part of the labor force in virtually every section of the five-state area, and in many localities their numbers predominate in certain segments of the labor market. This section examines the role that Chicanos play in the region's labor markets.

The Labor Force

Of the 4.7 million persons in the Southwest having Spanish surnames in 1970, 1.5 million were considered part of the labor force of the region. It should be understood that the phrase "labor force" in this usage is not intended to include all persons who are industrious, engaged in productive activities, or busy with worthwhile endeavors. It has a more limited meaning— that of defining a role many persons play in the economy. Essentially, the phrase includes those persons 16 years of age or more who are in the labor market, that is, who are employed or who seek employment, but it also includes persons who work in their own business or profession or who are engaged in unpaid work in family enterprises, such as farming—provided they work in such enterprises at least 15 hours a week. Such persons are workers for purposes of this analysis. Obviously, this definition leaves aside many persons who are fully engaged in the work of caring for their families at home, those who are involved in important voluntary activities in their communities, those engaged in illicit activities for profit, and others who may be involved in the economy as owners of productive facilities or landed properties.

Table 2.1 shows the extent to which Chicano workers are a part of the labor supply in the five southwestern states. The proportion they represent in each state's labor force has been a growing one over the years, especially in Texas and California.

TABLE 2.1. *Labor force of the Southwest, 1970*

(Persons age 16 and over; in thousands)

	All persons	Spanish surname	% labor force	SLSS*	% labor force
Southwest	14,739	1,514	10.3	2,088	14.2
Arizona	667	75	11.2	106	15.9
California	8,338	765	9.2	1,119	13.4
Colorado	911	68	7.4	93	10.3
New Mexico	358	92	25.8	122	34.1
Texas	4,465	514	11.5	648	14.5

Sources: U.S. Bureau of the Census, "Persons of Spanish Surname," *Census: 1970, Subject Reports*, PC(2)-1D, table 9, pp. 42–59. Idem, *Census: 1970, General Social and Economic Characteristics*, PC(1)-C4, *Arizona*, table 53, pp. 101–102; PC(1)-C6, *California*, table 53, pp. 395–396; PC(1)-C7, *Colorado*, table 53, pp. 150–151; PC(1)-C33, *New Mexico*, table 53, pp. 105–106; and PC(1)-C45, *Texas*, table 53, pp. 443–444.

*Spanish language-Spanish surname.

That Chicanos have different experiences than do most other persons in the labor markets of the Southwest is known to all who live in the region. Even casual visitors sense that Chicanos are a part of, but also apart from, much of the region's economic and social activity, and that the roles they have in the world of work do subtly, if not overtly, add to their apartness.

These facts and the widespread knowledge of them in the Southwest make recent governmental attention to Chicanos and their problems appear belated. This belated concern is made quite apparent in the *Manpower Report of the President* for 1973.[1] In that report, considerable presidential concern is expressed for how Spanish-speaking Americans are faring in the labor market.

There have been eleven annual manpower reports to the Congress since the first one in 1962. The reports prior to 1973

TABLE 2.2. *Labor-force participation rates, southwestern states, 1970* (% noninstitutional population)

| | All areas | | Urban | |
	Anglo	Spanish surname	Anglo	Spanish surname
				MALES 16+
Southwest	78.2	77.2	79.2	78.2
Arizona	74.7	78.3	75.7	78.7
California	78.0	79.0	78.7	79.5
Colorado	79.0	74.4	79.2	75.9
New Mexico	77.8	70.4	78.6	74.5
Texas	79.2	76.2	80.9	77.2
				FEMALES 16+
Southwest	41.2	36.7	42.6	38.0
Arizona	40.1	34.4	41.6	35.2
California	41.7	39.4	42.5	40.1
Colorado	42.8	36.6	44.3	38.2
New Mexico	39.2	32.5	40.8	35.9
Texas	40.2	34.2	42.5	35.8

Sources: U.S. Bureau of the Census, "Persons of Spanish Surname," *Census: 1970, Subject Reports*, PC(2)-1D, table 9, pp. 42–59. Idem, *Census: 1970, General Social and Economic Characteristics*, PC(1)-C4, *Arizona*, table 53, pp. 101–102; PC(1)-C6, *California*, table 53, pp. 395–396; PC(1)-C7, *Colorado*, table 53, pp. 150–151; PC(1)-C33, *New Mexico*, table 53, pp. 105–106; and PC(1)-C45, *Texas*, table 53, pp. 443–444.

| Rural nonfarm | | Rural farm | |
Anglo	Spanish surname	Anglo	Spanish surname
72.0	70.3	77.6	78.9
69.3	75.9	75.8	86.4
70.7	73.0	78.3	85.3
76.7	68.4	83.0	75.0
74.7	63.1	75.9	65.4
72.5	70.9	76.2	77.4
34.1	28.2	29.4	23.3
33.0	30.9	31.4	20.1
33.9	31.5	31.5	29.0
39.0	30.2	30.6	22.1
35.1	26.6	27.6	19.9
33.4	26.0	28.2	20.7

gave singular attention to the manpower problems of black workers, as these varied from year to year, with only occasional subhead notations devoted to the problems faced by the Spanish speaking. In 1973 this emphasis was reordered rather dramatically. That year, fully one-fourth of the text of the large annual report was devoted to "Spanish-speaking Americans: Their Manpower Problems and Opportunities," while fewer than two pages were devoted to the continuing problems of black workers. This transfer of emphasis came as though some formal decision had been made that the Spanish speaking were now to be considered "in" and blacks benignly "out" in government documents that focus our national concern on citizen problems. Whatever the case, the manpower problems confronted by the Spanish speaking, of which Chicanos are the largest component, can no longer be dismissed as a regional phenomenon; they have been pronounced by the president to be a national concern.

Labor-Force Participation

The Chicano labor-force participation rate, that is, the percentage of males over 16 years of age either employed or actively seeking employment, is very similar to that of Anglo males in the Southwest.[2] Table 2.2 presents the statistics.

The intrastate differences between Chicano rates and those for Anglo workers are, for the most part, less than interstate differences among Chicanos themselves (for example, their rate in New Mexico compared to that in the other states). But these interstate differences are most likely a consequence of the different age and rural-urban distributions prevailing in the various states. They suggest nothing about any significant difference in the work readiness of Chicanos compared to other groups of workers in any of the states.

Any differences in work readiness that do appear seem to be a function of age. (Table 2.3 presents participation rates by age for California and Texas. These two states together contain 85 percent of the Mexican American population of the Southwest.) Chicanos tend to enter the labor force at a later age than do Anglo workers. The widest differences in participation rates are found in the case of those 16–19 years old. By ages 20–24,

TABLE 2.3. *Labor-force participation rates by age and sex, California and Texas, 1970*

State	Surname	16–19 %	20–24 %	25–34 %	35–44 %	45–64 %
				Male		
California	Anglo	53.2	82.3	93.4	95.4	87.6
	Spanish	48.0	84.3	92.6	93.4	86.2
Texas	Anglo	49.2	83.9	95.2	96.0	88.4
	Spanish	41.8	82.8	92.9	93.5	85.4
				Female		
California	Anglo	35.9	58.0	46.5	50.6	47.6
	Spanish	30.2	50.7	41.9	45.5	40.4
Texas	Anglo	31.0	53.1	44.0	50.2	46.4
	Spanish	26.1	47.8	40.9	38.6	30.9

Sources: U.S. Bureau of the Census, "Persons of Spanish Surname," *Census: 1970, Subject Reports*, PC(2)-1D, table 9, pp. 42–59. Idem, *Census: 1970: Detailed Characteristics*, PC(1)-D6, *California*, table 165, pp. 1415–1429; and PC(1)-D45, *Texas*, table 165, pp. 1481–1492.

however, the Chicano workers are almost as active in the labor force as Anglo males at that age. From that point, their activity in the California labor force stays generally the same as that of Anglos, while in Texas their relative participation declines slightly through the older age groups.

The situation is significantly otherwise for Chicanas. Table 2.2 shows that their labor-force participation rates are consistently lower than those for Anglo females. In no case do Chicana participation rates come up to the rates for Anglo women—not among the urban, rural farm, or rural nonfarm population in any of the states. Although their participation in the labor force trails only slightly behind Anglo females in California (39.4 to 41.7 percent), the difference is roughly six percentage points in all other states of the region. This suggests that there are residual cultural factors still operating in Chicano families that tend to discourage the entry of females into work outside the home.

One such factor often mentioned in this connection is the notion of machismo—the role concept of the males as the exclusive provider for the family and the dominant head of the household. Within this framework, the man's "masculinity" is seen as reduced by the employment of his mate outside the household.

Table 2.3 shows that the labor-force participation of Mexican American females is substantially below that of Anglo females at all age levels. The greatest disparities occur in Texas, where Mexican American females have very low participation rates after age 35.

It is interesting to note that the participation figures for women not living with their husbands or who are unmarried are almost the same for Anglos and Chicanas. The incidence of Chicano families headed by females (13 percent) is slightly higher than is the case in all families but is only one-half that found among Negro families (25 percent).[3]

The tendency for Chicanas not to enter the labor force is most notable where there are children under 18 years of age in the family. Where there are no children under 18 years of age, Chicanas are as likely to be in the labor force as are other females.[4] One of the most significant developments in the labor-market experience of Mexican Americans in the last censual period is the way labor-force participation rates of females have increased, especially in urban areas. This development suggests that during the 1960's there was a considerable diminishing of cultural influences that once deterred Chicanas from seeking employment.

There were only slight increases in the labor-force participation rates of urban Chicano males from 1960 to 1970 (Colorado, where the rate jumped 5.1 percent, was an exception). But in each state, the rate for urban females moved dramatically upward, a movement ranging from a 7.7 percent increase in Texas to a 10.4 percent increase in Colorado. These are movements of major significance, indicating that Chicanas are tracking Anglo females in entering the labor force in large numbers and will soon have parity with them, if present trends continue.

The very highest rate of participation in the labor force for any group was found in the rural farm population of Arizona, where 86.4 percent of the males in the Chicano population are in the labor force, and the lowest rate was the 19.9 percent rate for females in the New Mexico rural farm Chicano population. Among the states with large Chicano populations, Texas and California, in the matter of labor-force participation as in many others, seem to represent the end bands of a spectrum depicting the breaking up of cultural ties that extend from Mexico to Texas and thence to California (see table 2.2).

Although Chicano males are represented in the labor force to the same extent as are other workers, only about three-fourths of them have full-year work, a smaller proportion than is the case for Anglo males.[5] Except for Arizona, where both groups of males have about the same extent of full employment, Chicanos generally lag from 7 to 10 percentage points behind Anglo males in this respect. This is undoubtedly one of the facts contributing to the lower median annual incomes of Chicanos, described in chapter 3.

The situation for females in the labor force is inclined even less toward full-year work. The percentage of Chicanas in full-year work ranges from 41 in Arizona to 50 in New Mexico. In the latter state this percentage is only slightly below that for Anglo females, but in the other states the proportion of Chicana workers who have full-year work trails Anglo female workers by 5–7 percent.

It should be observed here that the higher rate of less than full-year work for Chicanos is accounted for in part by the large representation they have in seasonal occupations. This fact in itself may tend to understate the overall unemployment rates for Chicanos, for the Bureau of Labor Statistics does not include in the labor force those seasonal workers who were not working or seeking work in the week of its monthly surveys. There are clearly many seasonal workers whose work experiences have convinced them that there are few job opportunities outside their usual seasonal work; hence they do not seek other work. Therefore, for parts of the year they are not counted as unemployed, even though they may wish very much to have year-round work.[6]

It should be observed that labor-force participation can be gauged in different ways. The census takes its measure by asking whether a person has worked in the preceding week, while in some Bureau of Labor Statistics surveys the question put to a respondent is whether he or she has worked at any time during the year. Different results are seen from these two perspectives. The 1973 *Manpower Report of the President* reports that 91.8 percent of Spanish-speaking American husbands in the United States (not just the Southwest) had work experience in 1970 but that only 61.8 percent worked full time the year round. This compares with the Anglo figures of 89.9 percent and 69.4 percent, respectively. Among wives of the Spanish speaking, 54.4 percent worked at some time during that year, but only 11.0 percent worked full time year round. These, again, compare to the figures for Anglo wives of 50.0 percent and 20.1 percent, respectively.

It goes without comment that labor-force participation rates are affected by rates of unemployment. As unemployment goes up in an area, there is a tendency for some Mexican American workers to become discouraged in their search for jobs and to withdraw from the labor force.

Unemployment

There are other uncertainties about labor-force data on Chicanos which, of course, come not only because of the already described definitional problems of identifying this population grouping but also because the only detailed data are from the decennial census and a few special surveys that have been made only within the last decade. There has never been the same continuing effort to collect information about Spanish-surname persons as has been the case for the Negro and nonwhite portions of the population.

Census reports show that, in the search for jobs, Chicanos fare less favorably than do Anglos. In 1970 their rate of unemployment in the five states ranged from 25 to over 100 percent larger than that of Anglos, from 4.2 percent for males in Arizona to 7.7 percent in Colorado, as shown in table 2.4.

The rates for Chicana workers were higher yet, ranging from 7.1 percent in Texas to 10.0 percent in California. The ratios of their rates to the Anglo female rates are approximately the same as those for males of the two states. Nonetheless, these rates and their ratios to Anglo rates did reflect an improvement in Chicano unemployment relative to that of Anglos in all five states over the Chicano unemployment status that prevailed at the time of

TABLE 2.4. *Unemployment rates, southwestern states,*
1960 and 1970

		Male			Female		
		Anglo %	Spanish surname %	SS/A	Anglo %	Spanish surname %	SS/A
Southwest	1960	4.5	8.0	1.8	5.1	9.7	1.9
	1970	4.4	6.2	1.4	5.5	8.7	1.6
Arizona	1960	4.3	6.2	1.4	4.5	8.1	1.8
	1970	3.4	4.2	1.2	4.3	7.7	1.8
California	1960	5.3	7.7	1.5	5.9	11.2	1.9
	1970	5.5	7.2	1.3	6.0	10.0	1.7
Colorado	1960	3.4	9.5	2.8	3.8	8.9	2.3
	1970	3.5	7.7	2.1	4.3	7.7	1.8
New Mexico	1960	3.7	10.3	2.8	4.8	8.6	1.8
	1970	3.4	7.0	2.1	5.7	8.5	1.5
Texas	1960	3.3	8.2	2.5	3.7	8.2	2.2
	1970	2.4	4.9	2.0	3.8	7.1	1.9

Sources: U.S. Bureau of the Census, "Persons of Spanish Surname," *Census:*
1970, Subject Reports, PC(2)-1D, table 9, pp. 42–59. Idem, *Census: 1970,*
General Social and Economic Characteristics, PC(1)-C4, *Arizona*, table 53,
pp. 101–102; PC(1)-C6, *California*, table 53, pp. 395–396; PC(1)-C7, *Colo-*
rado, table 53, pp. 150–151; PC(1)-C33, *New Mexico*, table 53, pp. 105–106;
and PC(1)-C45, *Texas*, table 53, pp. 443–444. Idem, "Persons of Spanish
Surname," *Census: 1960, Subject Reports*, PC(2)-1B, table 6, pp. 38–49.
Idem, *Census: 1960*, vol. 1, *Characteristics of the Population*, pt. 4,
Arizona, table 115, pp. 186–191; pt. 6, *California*, table 115, pp. 601–621;
pt. 7, *Colorado*, table 115, pp. 257–262; pt. 33, *New Mexico*, table 115, pp.
200–203; and pt. 45, *Texas*, table 115, pp. 785–800.

Note: 1960 data for persons 14+, 1970 data for persons 16+.

the 1960 census.[7] The improved ratios occurred for both males and females but were most notable for males in Colorado and New Mexico, where the ratios fell from 2.8 in 1960 to 2.1 in 1970.

Unemployment rates prevailing within the states in 1970 were highest in the cases of the Chicano male rural nonfarm workers and the female rural farm workers. The highest rate in any state for any group of workers was 12.6 percent for Chicana workers in Colorado's rural farm population.[8]

Table 2.5 compares Spanish-surname and Anglo unemployment by age group. Generally, the best relative experience of Chicanos occurs before age 25. Their comparative experience is least satisfactory in Texas, where middle-aged and older Anglos had very low rates of unemployment in 1970.

Manpower Training

These unemployment rates somewhat understate actual unemployment for all groups of workers, since unemployed persons who are enrolled in some federally sponsored manpower training programs are not counted as unemployed. This would be of no statistical consequence in interpreting the relative standings of the groups if all population groups were proportionately enrolled in such programs. Such is not the case.

Spanish-surname persons are enrolled in the various work and training programs in numbers heavily disproportionate to their size in the population of each state. A breakdown provided by the Manpower Administration (now called Employment and Training Administration) of enrollment in all five southwestern states shows that during fiscal year 1972 there were 68,700 Chicano enrollees compared to only 52,000 Anglo enrollees.[9] Clearly, were it not for these programs, Chicano unemployment rates would stand in an even more unfavorable ratio to the Anglo rates than the above figures indicate. The number of Chicanos enrolled in manpower programs in the Southwest during 1972 was equal to two-thirds the number of Chicanos unemployed in that region. Thus, the decline during 1960–1970 in Chicano unemployment relative to that of Anglos (table 2.4) is probably accounted for by greater enrollment of the former in manpower programs.

TABLE 2.5. *Unemployment rates by age and sex,
California and Texas, 1970*

State	Surname	16–19 %	20–24 %	25–34 %	35–44 %	45–64 %
		Male				
California	Anglo	14.1	10.4	4.3	3.6	4.4
	Spanish	15.2	10.5	6.0	5.3	5.8
	(SS/A)	(1.1)	(1.0)	(1.4)	(1.4)	(1.3)
Texas	Anglo	9.5	4.5	1.7	1.3	1.7
	Spanish	12.1	6.9	3.3	3.3	4.2
	(SS/A)	(1.3)	(1.5)	(1.9)	(2.5)	(2.5)
		Female				
California	Anglo	14.7	8.1	5.6	5.4	4.9
	Spanish	14.9	10.3	9.2	9.3	9.0
	(SS/A)	(1.0)	(1.6)	(1.6)	(1.7)	(1.8)
Texas	Anglo	11.3	5.8	3.5	2.6	2.5
	Spanish	13.9	8.3	5.3	6.0	5.3
	(SS/A)	(1.2)	(1.4)	(1.5)	(2.3)	(2.1)

Sources: U.S. Bureau of the Census, "Persons of Spanish Surname," *Census:
1970, Subject Reports*, PC(2)-1D, table 9, pp. 42–59. Idem, *Census: 1970,
Detailed Characteristics*, PC(1)-D4, *Arizona*, table 164, pp. 342–351;
PC(1)-D6, *California*, table 164, pp. 1387–1414; PC(1)-D7, *Colorado*, table
164, pp. 435–442; PC(1)-D33, *New Mexico*, table 164, pp. 345–352; and
PC(1)-D45, *Texas*, table 164, pp. 1459–1480.

Mexican Americans have become increasingly well represented in federally sponsored manpower programs over the last few years. Among the southwestern states in 1972, their representation in these programs ranged from 31 percent in California to 57 percent in New Mexico.[10]

Beginning in 1966 the Department of Labor and the Office of Economic Opportunity recognized that the manpower problems of Chicanos were of a kind to warrant establishing specialized programs differing from other categorical manpower programs sponsored by the federal government. Because of cultural differences, language barriers, the frequent isolation of Chicanos in barrios apart from urban and rural communities, and the absence of existing labor-market information systems effectively reaching them, these agencies launched a manpower program operated by and directed by Chicanos. This program is known as Operation SER—an acronym for Service, Employment, and Redevelopment.

The program, which was initially aimed solely at disadvantaged Chicanos in a few selected areas of the Southwest, was steadily extended up to 1973 to cover broader geographical areas, some outside the Southwest. The U.S. Department of Health, Education, and Welfare joined in helping to expand the services of Operation SER, and in 1973 the contract for these services totaled $18 million covering activities in a total of thirty-eight cities. The contract has been with two long-established Mexican American organizations: the American GI Forum, founded by a group of veterans after World War II to combat discrimination against Chicanos in schools and elsewhere, and the League of United Latin American Citizens, an organization largely composed of Chicano businessmen and civic leaders.

Operation SER has been distinguished from most other manpower programs in that it has a largely bilingual staff operating under a national office, with local offices governed by boards of directors drawn from the communities served. In addition to occupational training, job-placement assistance, counseling, and adult basic education, the program offers instruction in English as a second language to many of its enrollees. Its emphasis is intended to be on training workers to qualify for local job openings rather than persuading employers to employ SER trainees. However, in some cases it serves as a recruitment channel for

companies and public agencies able and willing to employ
Chicano workers. In the 1972 fiscal year the program was cred-
ited with training 2,500 enrollees and developing jobs for 2,800
others.[11] Nonetheless, this number of trainees represented only
1 percent of the total enrollment of Spanish-speaking persons in
national manpower programs during that year.

Manpower programs, including SER, appear to have served
Chicanos about as well as they have served other disadvantaged
groups—fairly effectively in tight labor markets and ineffectively
in loose labor markets when unemployment rates are generally
high. The Public Employment Program under the Emergency
Employment Act of 1971 has been the most helpful, although on
a very modest scale.[12]

Although Chicanos appear to be heavily represented in most
of the federally sponsored categorical manpower work and training programs, all of which were created during the past decade,
they have not fared as well in longer-established public and
private vocational training programs.

The 1970 *Census* provides information on the number of persons 16–64 years of age who in 1970 had less than 15 years of
schooling but had received some vocational training. From these
data it is clear that Chicanos received notably less vocational
training than their counterparts in either the Anglo or the Negro
population. This was true for both males and females in each of
the southwestern states, suggesting that this important factor is a
determinant of the occupational position of Chicanos. In California, for instance, where 37 percent of Anglo males had received
vocational training (as had 32.1 percent of the Negro males),
only 23 percent of the Chicanos had the benefit of this training.
The situation was similarly disproportionate among California
females, with the comparable percentages for each group being
28, 29, and 18. And, it should be noted, it was in California that
Chicanos fared best among the states with regard to the extent of
their vocational training.

The poor representation of Chicanos in general vocational
training is also evident in the formal trade union apprenticeship
programs. In recent years the federal government and some
states have tried by various devices to increase the entry of
minority workers into union apprenticeship programs. The Apprenticeship Information Reports which some unions are required to make to the Equal Employment Opportunity Com-

mission (EEOC) provide a partial reading of the effectiveness of these efforts. Whereas Negro workers constitute a much higher percentage among apprentices than they do in the membership of the reporting unions, the same is not true for "Spanish Americans" (as defined by EEOC surveys), who have less of proportionate showing in apprenticeship programs (3.1 percent) than they have in the total memberships of the referral unions that administer the programs (3.9 percent).[13] This suggests that Chicanos more frequently become journeymen through informal channels. Such representation as they do have in both union membership and apprenticeship is largest in the roofing and trowel trades (the last often referred to as the "mud trades"), not the mechanical trades. There appears to be for Spanish Americans an inverse relationship between skill level of an occupation and the participation they have in it. The same, of course, holds for Negro workers.

The Search for Jobs

It is not possible to learn from *Census* reports how workers secure their jobs. A few surveys have been made of this subject in various localities. The five-year Manpower Administration longitudinal study of the national labor-market experience of selected groups yields important information, but it does not show how the manner in which Chicanos enter the labor market differs from that of other workers.[14] As part of the 1970 *Census of Population and Housing*, special census employment surveys were made in several dozen areas of the country. In the final report, titled "Employment Profiles of Selected Low-Income Areas," five of the surveys provide detailed information on Chicanos within the surveyed cities.[15] Although information is only on Chicanos living in low-income areas, this sample represents a substantial part of their total number. The survey shows the principal job-seeking methods used by different groups of workers.[16] In the five cities it can be generalized that Chicanos made less use of the state employment services than did other workers, that they more frequently applied directly to employers, and that they were more apt than other workers to rely on friends and relatives for their employment. Direct application to employers was by far the most common method of job seeking.

Registering with a union for employment was one of the methods practiced the least.[17]

Significance of Chicano Labor Supply

Figures given at the outset of this section show that Chicanos constitute a substantial portion of the labor supply in the Southwest. In some localities, such as parts of South Texas and southern California, they represent a rapidly growing proportion of the local labor force, and in some cases their numbers predominate in the local labor supply. The reasons for this are both historical and economic. As observed in the preceding section, the tremendous disparities in wage levels and expectations between the United States and Mexico provide a persistent inducement for Mexican nationals to migrate to the United States. These same disparities also provide an attractive inducement to many U.S. firms, especially those making labor-intensive products, to locate their plants on the Mexican side of the border in industrial zones provided by the Mexican government. These firms are able to use lower-paid Mexican nationals as workers, provided their products are not made for sale in Mexico. Such plants no longer need to be located in the twelve-mile zone adjacent to the border but can also be in the interior of Mexico. United States Tariff regulations encourage such plant locations by treating the products as only partially manufactured goods for purposes of levying import duties. For example, an assembled electric appliance would not be regarded as a finished product if part of its wiring was left for completion in the United States.

Mexico thus continues to contribute in four ways to the labor supply of this country: through a steady flow of emigration; by the daily commuting of large numbers of workers who reside in Mexico (who under a legal fiction are treated as U.S. residents); by the covert and unlawful entry of unknown but enormous numbers of undocumented workers; and through its so-called Border Industrialization Program, whereby large numbers of low-paid workers who have gravitated to northern Mexico are made potentially available, through illegal immigration, to U.S. manufacturers for labor-intensive operations. It is very probable that many Mexican workers now acquire their basic introduction to and training in the ways of U.S. employers and industrial

operations through this last process, before taking other means
of becoming an acknowledged addition to the U.S. labor force.
Whatever the case, U.S. trade unions have long regarded the
Border Industrialization Program as one that results in the ex-
port of jobs, speaking critically of it as the "Hong Kongization"
of the border.[18] Certainly the program must act as a further
depressant on the wages of domestic workers who are located
near border areas and must compete in the very fluid labor
markets which are characteristic of those areas. This effect will
be discussed further in the next chapter.

It is a well known, although unresearched, fact that the men's
and women's clothing and millinery industries, as well as other
labor-intensive industries, have tended to move toward the
Southwest from their historical locations in the East. A major
factor in this movement has been the existence in the Southwest
of a low-wage labor supply consisting of Mexican Americans,
border commuters, and immigrants from Mexico. Undoubtedly,
employers have found attractive the inherent difficulties of un-
ionizing such a labor supply. These difficulties are illustrated by
the year-and-a-half strike for union recognition which was conducted by the employees of Farah, Inc., the nation's largest
manufacturer of men's slacks.[19] The company's plants, which are
in Texas and New Mexico near the Mexican border in most
cases, employ over 10,000 workers, 90 percent of whom are
Chicanos and 85 percent women. The fact that the strike ended
with the formal recognition of a union bargaining agent represents a symbolic and substantive achievement for organized
labor and the Chicano workers, but this accomplishment can
hardly be considered a harbinger of future success in the organization of the border labor supply—a supply which appears to
have unlimited elasticity at or near the prevailing federal
minimum wage.

3. Income and Earnings

Chicanos have substantially smaller incomes than Anglos in the Southwest, but they have larger incomes than blacks. Improvements in Chicano income are dependent upon better schooling (quantity and quality), a reduced rate of immigration from Mexico, and a decline in discrimination.

Family Income

Looking first at the United States as a whole, the median income of Mexican-origin families in 1970 was $7,120. This is 70 percent of the figure for all white (including Mexican-origin) families in the country and 113 percent of Negro family income.[1]

In the Southwest, median family income of the Spanish-surname population in 1969 was $7,080, compared to $10,750 and $6,320 for Anglo and Negro families in the region.[2] The Spanish-surname figure is 66 percent of the Anglo median and 112 percent of the median income for black families.[3]

These income data refer to families where the head worked part time or only part of the year as well as to those families headed by full-time, full-year workers. When we look only at the latter, the relative position of Mexican American families is slightly better. The median income of Mexican-origin families headed by year-round, full-time workers was $8,950 in 1970, 74 percent of the figure for all white families in the United States.[4] It is evident that the high incidence of part-time or part-year work among Chicanos adversely affects their incomes in comparison to those of Anglos—57 percent of the Mexican-origin heads of families work full time the year round compared to 66 percent of all white heads.[5] On the other hand, Negroes and Chicanos have equal incomes when full-time, year-round family heads are compared, in contrast to the substantial advantage which exists for Chicanos over Negroes when all family heads are compared. Since only 51 percent of the Negro family heads (one-third of whom are women) work full time and year round, it is clear that the great incidence of part-time and part-year work among Negro family heads (particularly females) is the major factor contributing to their family-income disadvantage relative to Mexican Americans.

It should be noted that Chicano family income is spread over more persons than is true of either Anglo or Negro family income, because of the larger average size of Chicano families (see chapter 1). When incomes are adjusted for family size, the comparative advantage of Anglos increases while Chicano and black incomes become approximately equal.

Large families as well as other factors tend to restrict the labor-force activity of Mexican American wives (see chapter 2). Even when they do work, their contribution to family income is comparatively small—little more than an average of $2,000 in 1970.[6] On the other hand, almost 15 percent of the Spanish-surname families in the Southwest were headed by females in 1969, and the median income of these families was only $3,570.[7]

Mexican Americans do enjoy an income advantage over blacks but they have substantially lower incomes than most other ethnic populations in the United States. Table 3.1 compares the median incomes of families headed by persons of various ethnic origins. No attempt has been made to adjust these incomes for any of the factors which produce income variation—age, education, location, and so forth; instead, the data serve as a very general reference point from which inquiry into the relative income experience of Chicanos can be made. The median income of Spanish-origin families in the United States (almost 60 percent are of Mexican origin) is by far the lowest of any of the ethnic groups included in table 3.1. Among the groups separately enumerated, the Irish incomes are closest to those of Spanish-origin families, and the differential enjoyed by the former is almost $2,500. Aside from families of Russian origin, who have particularly large incomes, the median incomes of the other five ethnic groups in table 3.1 are all between $8,100 and $8,900. The substantial drop to the median Spanish-origin income of $5,640 demonstrates that the appellation "disadvantaged" is appropriate for the Chicano and other Spanish American populations.

Among the groups usually thought of as disadvantaged, Chicanos enjoy a midway position on income measures—better than that of blacks, American Indians, and Puerto Ricans but

TABLE 3.1. *Median family income by ethnic origin of head, United States, 1968*

Origin	Number of family heads (in thousands)	Median family income
Russian	598	$11,550
Polish	1,149	8,850
Italian	1,924	8,810
German	5,674	8,610
English	4,997	8,320
Irish	3,639	8,130
Other	22,051	7,670
Not reported	4,657	7,260
Spanish	1,927	5,640
Total	46,616	

Sources: U.S. Bureau of the Census, "Characteristics of the Population by Ethnic Origin: November 1969," *Current Population Reports*, P-20, no. 221, table 14, p. 22.

inferior to that of Asian groups and Cubans. In 1971, Mexican-origin family income was $1,300 larger than that of Puerto Ricans but $1,900 less than Cuban family income.[8] Table 3.2 shows that Asian American families have much larger incomes than Mexican Americans and that Japanese families have larger incomes than Anglos as well.

TABLE 3.2. *Median family income of selected population groups, California, 1969*

Group	Median income
Japanese	$12,390
Anglo	11,550
Chinese	10,920
Filipino	9,120
Spanish surname	8,430
American Indian	7,950
Negro	7,840

Sources: U.S. Bureau of the Census, "Negro Population," *Census: 1970, Subject Reports,* PC(2)-1B, table 9, pp. 143–152; "Persons of Spanish Surname," PC(2)-1D, table 12, pp. 81–83; "American Indians," PC(2)-1F, table 9, pp. 120–128; and "Japanese, Chinese, and Filipinos in the United States," PC(2)-1G, table 9, pp. 42–45, table 24, pp. 101–104, table 39, pp. 160–163. Idem, *Census: 1970, Detailed Characteristics,* PC(1)-D6, *California,* table 198, pp. 2345–2353.

Regional Differences

There are large differences between urban and rural incomes for Mexican Americans as for all other populations. Spanish-surname urban families in the Southwest had median incomes of $7,390 in 1969 compared to $5,220 for rural families.[9] The effects of the small rural incomes are not substantial for the total group, how-

TABLE 3.3. *Median income of Spanish-surname families, southwestern states, 1969*

State	Median income	Spanish surname as % of Anglo	Spanish surname as % of Negro
Arizona	$7,350	74	129
California	8,430	73	113
Colorado	6,930	69	97
New Mexico	5,890	67	113
Texas	5,600	58	105

Sources: U.S. Bureau of the Census, "Persons of Spanish Surname," *Census: 1970, Subject Reports*, PC(2)-1D, table 12, pp. 81–83. Idem, *Census: 1970, General Social and Economic Characteristics*, PC(1)-C4, *Arizona*, table 57, pp. 109–110; PC(1)-C6, *California*, table 57, pp. 403–404; PC(1)-C7, *Colorado*, table 57, pp. 158–159; PC(1)-C33, *New Mexico*, table 57, pp. 134–135; and PC(1)-C45, *Texas*, table 57, pp. 451–452.

ever, since 86 percent of all Chicanos in the Southwest live in urban areas. This fact in no way ameliorates the plight of the migratory farm labor force discussed below, in chapter 5.

Turning to state differences, table 3.3 shows the variation which exists in Chicano absolute and relative incomes among the five southwestern states. The two states with the largest Chicano populations, California and Texas, are at the high and low extremes, respectively, of income variation for this group. Since these two states contain 85 percent of the Spanish-surname populations of the Southwest, it is clear that when one generalizes about Mexican American income (or other experiences) in the Southwest, or in the entire United States for that matter, he is dealing largely with an average of the California and Texas experience. The income and other experiences of the Spanish-surname population in other states are qualitatively important but have little influence on summary measures for the entire Southwest.

The relatively favorable income experience of California Chicanos corresponds with the fact that schooling achievement, in terms of school years completed, is also greatest in California. Another factor which may contribute to the California advantage is the more compressed wage structure which exists in that state. For example, wages of manual workers are closer to those of professional workers in California than in Texas—for all persons, not just Chicanos—and since the latter tend to be employed predominantly as manual workers, this wage-structure artifact produces a favorable impact on the California incomes of this group.[10] Another factor is that many Chicanos in Texas are concentrated in South Texas, which is a low-income region of that state.[11] In contrast, income variation within California is not very great.

Interestingly, the best Mexican American income experience is now found outside the Southwest. The 1969 median income of the 35,000 Illinois families of Mexican origin was $9,300; in Michigan it was $9,400 for the 13,400 Mexican-origin families who lived there. These figures are more than $1,000 larger than the comparable California statistics.[12]

Similar results are obtained with male incomes for metropolitan areas. Mexican-origin males in 1969 had their largest income in Detroit—a median of $8,000. Median Mexican-origin incomes (males) for other metropolitan areas include San Francisco, $6,580; Orange County, California, $6,580; Los Angeles, $6,150; Denver, $5,410; and Houston, $5,380.

Almost one-third of Illinois's Mexican-origin population was born in Mexico, and almost one-fifth was born in Texas. Less of Michigan's Mexican-origin population was born in Mexico (12 percent), but 29 percent of it was born in Texas.[13] Apparently, there is a stream of migration from Mexico and Texas to Chicago and Detroit (often with intermediate stops in midwestern agriculture), which enables a small number of Chicanos to improve their incomes through employment in the automobile industry in Detroit and the steel industry in the Chicago area. Chicano employment in these heavy manufacturing industries dates from World War I and now appears to be spreading to other sectors.[14]

As shown by table 3.3 Chicano income exceeds that of blacks in all states of the Southwest except Colorado, where the black population—which is quite small in Colorado—has obtained one of its better relative income positions.

Individual Incomes

Thus far we have looked at the status of Chicanos chiefly in terms of family income. Since the household or family is the basic economic and social unit in our society, a great deal of importance attaches to family income. If one is interested, however, in the labor-market experience of individuals, Chicanos or any other identifiable group, individual income is a more appropriate concept than family income. (Statistics on *earnings*, the most useful measure of labor-market experience, are not generally available for the Spanish-surname population.) Table 3.4 presents median incomes for those Spanish-surname persons in the Southwest, aged 25–64, who had incomes in 1969.

Comparison of individual Chicano incomes to those of Anglos produces results similar to those obtained with family-income comparisons. This is particularly true for males. Both male (age 25–64) and family incomes for Chicanos were 66 percent of their Anglo counterparts in the Southwest for 1969. Variations among the five southwestern states are also similar for male and family incomes.

Mexican American females have an income experience which is roughly comparable to that of males, although female relative incomes are less than those of males in Arizona and Colorado. Interestingly, the income of Chicano females in California is only 86 percent of the median income of black females in that state. In turn, the median income of black females in California is almost 85 percent of that of Anglo females.

Intergenerational Change

One of the explanations offered for the disadvantaged status of Chicanos is the fact that much of this population is relatively new to the United States—as a result of immigration from Mexico during this century—and has a cultural heritage which differs from that existing in this country. Comparisons among the different generations of Mexican Americans are, consequently, of great interest. If the experience of this group is strongly influenced by its newness and cultural heritage, one might expect improvements between the first and second generations,

TABLE 3.4. *Median income of Spanish-surname persons, age 25–64, southwestern states, 1969*

| | Male | | |
	Median income	% of Anglo median	% of Negro median
Southwest	$6,220	66	
Arizona	6,590	75	
California	7,200	72	108
Colorado	6,350	72	
New Mexico	5,510	64	
Texas	4,880	58	104

Sources: U.S. Bureau of the Census, "Persons of Spanish Surname," *Census: 1970, Subject Reports*, PC(2)-1D, table 9, pp. 42–59; and "Negro Population," PC(2)-1B, table 4, pp. 30–39. Idem, *Census: 1970, Detailed Characteristics*, PC(1)-D1, *U.S. Summary*, table 344, p. 1640.

the second and third, and so forth. Table 3.5 presents the facts for individual incomes.

The "newness" hypothesis receives mixed support from table 3.5. The incomes of first-generation (born in Mexico) persons are much lower than those of the second and third generations (the second and third columns, respectively, of table 3.5), and this does adversely affect the experience of the total group. On the other hand, the incomes of third-generation Chicanos (column three also encompasses later generations) are not better than those of the second generation—at least for males. This result exists despite slightly greater schooling for the third-generation group—for example, third-generation males, age 35–44, have almost a year more schooling than their second-generation counterparts.

It is not possible to analyze these generational facts from the gross census data which are available. Perhaps the third-

	Female	
Median income	% of Anglo median	% of Negro median
$2,530	67	
2,270	65	
2,940	72	86
2,200	66	
2,090	64	
2,070	62	101

generation persons who continue to live in the older—and low income—Hispano settlements in Colorado and New Mexico have an adverse income effect. Third-generation males do have much larger mean than median incomes, which suggests that some fraction of this group is receiving quite large incomes.

In any event, the disadvantaged status of Mexican Americans is not due entirely to the large number of Mexican-born persons in the group. Even third-generation males, age 35–44, had only 77 percent of the median income of Anglo males (age 25–64) in 1969.

Poverty

The incidence of poverty-level incomes among Chicanos is much greater than among Anglos but is not as great as among black

TABLE 3.5. *Mean income of Spanish-surname persons in the Southwest by nativity class, 1969*

Sex and age class		Born in Mexico	Natives of Mexican parentage	Natives of native parentage
Male	25–34	$5,386	$6,520	$6,450
	35–44	5,983	7,220	7,230
Female	25–34	2,630	2,930	3,020
	35–44	2,530	2,920	3,190

Source: U.S. Bureau of the Census, "Persons of Spanish Surname," *Census: 1970, Subject Reports*, PC(2)-1D, table 9, pp. 42–59.

families. In 1969, 33 percent of all Spanish-surname families in the Southwest had incomes of less than $5,000 ($5,000 is slightly greater than one-half the median income of all Southwest families for 1969), compared to 16 percent of Anglo families and 39 percent of black families.[15]

Great regional variation in the extent of poverty exists for the Chicano population, just as it does for blacks. In California, 23 percent of all Spanish-surname families had incomes of less than $5,000 in 1969 compared to 44 percent in Texas.[16] This income measure of poverty, of course, does not take into account differences between the two states in prices or general standards of living; adjustments for these considerations would lessen the California-Texas difference somewhat. On the other hand, public assistance policies in the two states exacerbate the welfare effects of the poverty difference. In California, 14 percent of all Spanish-surname families received public assistance or public welfare incomes in 1969, with an average money income from this source of $1,660. The comparable figures for Texas were 9 percent and $930.[17] The incidence of Chicano poverty is much greater, and its amelioration through public policy much less, in Texas than in California.

Some Explanations

AGE DIFFERENCES

Income is positively correlated with age in our society, at least through the middle age ranges, and it could be that differences between the age distribution of Chicanos and others account for some of the income differences shown above. Detailed age adjustments did not have much of an effect on the income experience of this group in 1959, however,[18] and the adjustments which were possible using the broad age groups (for Spanish-surname persons) of the 1970 *Census* did not raise the income of Spanish-surname persons relative to Anglos by more than .01 for any of the results presented in this chapter. Fine age adjustments could have slightly larger impacts, but this is not very likely. While there are differences between the Anglo and Chicano age distributions, they tend to be offsetting. The low proportion of Chicanos in the older age categories (55 and up), where earnings tend to be low, are offset by a high proportion of Chicanos in the younger ages (16–24), where earnings are also low.

The distinctiveness of the Chicano age distribution is a result of immigration and birth patterns. If the high birthrate of this population were to be reduced in this decade, the resulting relative concentration of the population in the prime earning ages would be advantageous for raising income for the subsequent 20 to 30 years.

EDUCATIONAL DIFFERENCES

Table 3.6 presents income data by school years completed for males 25 and over, 1971. Many readers will probably be surprised to learn that Mexican Americans who have 8 years of schooling or less earn substantially more than other persons with the same amount of schooling and that even through 12 years of schooling, Chicano incomes are more than 90 percent of their

TABLE 3.6. *Median income of Mexican-origin and all males by school years completed, age 25 and up, United States, 1971*

School years completed	Mexican origin	All persons	MO/AP
0–4	$3,960	$ 2,950	1.34
5–7	5,650	4,240	1.33
8	6,140	5,470	1.12
9–11	7,130	7,570	.94
12	8,420	9,090	.93
13+	9,150	11,890	.77

Source: U.S. Bureau of the Census, "Households and Families, by Type: March 1972," *Current Population Reports*, P-20, no. 237, table 8, p. 8.

total population counterparts. What happens after 12 years of schooling is unknown. The last row of table 3.6, which provides data for those with more than 13 years of schooling, compares to some extent apples and oranges: Chicanos with 13 and 14 years of schooling are mixed with total population persons who have greater amounts, so that the .77 relative income of Chicanos reflects differences in the distribution of the two groups as well as earnings differences between Chicanos and others with the same amount of education.

These income ratios for the various schooling classes are more favorable to Mexican Americans than those reported by the 1960 *Census of Population*.[19] Recently published reports of the 1970 *Census* tend to confirm current trends.[20] Careful analysis of the 1960–1970 gains in Chicano relative income for different amounts of schooling should prove interesting and useful. It is evident that Chicanos with limited amounts of schooling (less

than 12 years) do not now have difficulty competing with Anglos
and blacks who also have limited schooling. Most of this competition occurs in manual job markets where Chicanos may be
benefiting from stereotyped notions about their high productivity in these markets at the expense of low-productivity
stereotypes for nonmanual jobs.

Turning to more general comparisons, how is it that the relative income of all Mexican American males is .70 (compared to
all whites) if at most schooling levels their relative income is
above .90? The answer has already been suggested by the com-
ments on those with more than 13 years of schooling—many
more Mexican Americans than others are distributed over the
lower range of the schooling ladder.

Walter Fogel calculated the effect of the low distribution of
Chicano schooling on their relative income for 1959 and found
that 56 percent of the California income difference between
Chicanos and Anglos could be explained by the low schooling of
the former.[21] In Texas, schooling accounted for 47 percent of the
difference. In short, much of the low-income position of
Chicanos is associated with their limited schooling.

While much of the Chicano-Anglo income difference may be
associated with low schooling of the former, it would be a mistake to conclude that greater schooling will solve the income and
other labor-market problems of this group. In the first place
there is a delayed response of income to education in our society. The income benefits of education do not occur immediately.
Second, there is the matter of schooling quality. The Coleman
report, also known as the report *Equality of Educational Opportunity* of 1966, measured the achievement levels of Mexican
Americans as more than three grade levels below those of whites
in the metropolitan Northeast.[22] Little information is available
about the connection between quality of schooling and labor-
market income, but, presumably, the lower school achievement
of Chicanos would have at least a slightly adverse impact on their
incomes after equality in terms of years completed has been
achieved. Third, many factors other than schooling operate in
the labor market to affect incomes. One of these, discrimination,
is much spotlighted, and there are many others, including occupational interests and work motivation. As the educational attainments of Chicanos approach that of Anglos, the other
income-producing characteristics of the two groups must con-

verge before income equality can be achieved. This is beginning to be seen rather clearly for nonwhites, who, in some regions, are very near Anglos in terms of school years completed but are far below them in terms of income.

There is some quantitative support for a cautious view of the gains which can be made by Chicanos through greater schooling. To get at this matter, the effects of low Chicano schooling on their relative incomes in 1969 were computed, using the same method employed to obtain the 1959 results cited above. The 1969 results were that schooling differences accounted for 43 percent of the male income difference between Chicanos and Anglos in California and 51 percent in Texas. These compare to 56 and 47 percent, respectively, in 1959. During the 1960's, Mexican American (male) relative income in California stayed the same but relative schooling rose, causing the explanatory value of the latter to fall. In Texas, Mexican American relative income increased faster than the relative schooling, so that at the end of the decade schooling deficiencies explained a larger part of the now smaller income difference. We believe that the California experience will become typical for most of the remainder of this century. The "explanatory" value of schooling will fall as Chicano schooling advances more rapidly, in relative terms, than Chicano income.

Additional evidence is provided by failure of a human-capital model to explain earnings of this group. Jonathan King developed a wage equation for the work force of the United States (by city) which included schooling, vocational training, and age as independent variables and then found that Spanish-origin earnings are 14 percent larger than is predicted using Spanish-origin schooling, training, and age variables in the wage equation. On the other hand, black earnings are 19 percent less than is predicted by the wage equation.[23] The explanation for these seemingly contradictory results is that Mexican and other Spanish Americans are able to obtain many fairly well paid manual jobs despite their very low schooling while blacks, with much more schooling, obtain only the same, or slightly inferior, jobs. Thus, a human-capital formulation suggests labor-market discrimination against blacks and reverse discrimination in favor of Spanish-speaking groups. We suggest, instead, that a human-capital equation, with its heavy emphasis on schooling, is simply inadequate to explain more than gross variation in wages. As already indicated, we expect Chicano schooling, in relative terms, to rise faster than earnings. If so, human-capital equations in the future will suggest discrimination against Chicanos as well as against blacks; but, until our understanding of wage variation improves, alternative explanations of the low earnings of both groups cannot be ruled out.

The point of this discussion is not to disparage public or private attempts to raise the educational attainment of Chicanos. Given the gap between Chicano and Anglo schooling, many benefits should result from these attempts. Nevertheless, it must be recognized that other factors are also important and will become increasingly so as the schooling of this group improves.

OTHER FACTORS

Three other factors which contribute to the low earnings of Chicanos can be mentioned. It is important to recognize that these factors exist even though no attempt has been made to assess their impacts precisely.

1. Even though Mexican-origin persons lived in parts of the Southwest long before Anglo settlers arrived, this population group does include a larger proportion of immigrants and persons who had immigrant parents. In 1970, immigrants were 16 percent of the Spanish-surname population in the Southwest (the existence of illegal immigration suggests that the true proportion is much larger), and persons born of immigrant parents were 29 percent, together comprising a "foreign stock" which was 45 percent of the total Spanish-surname population.[24] This is much larger than the 17 percent foreign-stock proportion which prevailed for the total United States population in 1970.

There are obvious implications here for earning income. Lack of information about market institutions as well as the handicaps of noncitizenship and language problems adversely affect the labor-market experience of immigrants. In addition, most Mexican immigrants have been poorly schooled, unskilled workers who have had to accept low-skilled, low-wage employment.[25]

One result of this sizable foreign-born component of the Mexican American population has been to reduce average incomes for the group as a whole, directly through the low incomes of the immigrants themselves (see table 3.5) and indirectly through the effect of their competition on the incomes of native-born Mexican Americans. A 1965 study found that the average manufacturing wage in Laredo, Texas, a border city which is 80 percent Chicano, was just 50 percent of the state average for manufacturing. Furthermore, alien commuters were paid less than resident workers for similar work, and wages relative to statewide averages were much better in skilled occupations, which could not utilize the immigrant or commuter labor supply, than in unskilled ones.[26] These kinds of effects will continue as long as immigrants are a large component of the Chicano population.

2. There are heavy concentrations of Chicanos near the United States-Mexican border, particularly in South Texas, where incomes of all persons tend to be low. For example, in 1972 the average hourly earnings of maintenance carpenters in San Antonio (South Texas) were only 64 percent of those in Houston ($3.09 versus $4.84).[27] Chicano incomes in Texas would benefit from greater dispersion of this population throughout the state. This problem of population concentration near the border is, of course, closely connected to the immigration problem. Migration of Chicanos from the border regions to other parts of the United States tends to be offset by replacement immigration from Mexico, so that the effect of domestic migration on population concentration and income is retarded.

3. Various forms of labor-market discrimination undoubtedly have an adverse impact on Chicano incomes. Two recent studies have estimated the magnitude of this discrimination. One of them estimated discrimination against fully employed Chicano males in the Southwest, who were ages 20–40 in 1960, at 44 percent of the existing income difference between Anglos and Chicanos.[28] The second study was limited to Austin, Texas (1969), where the estimated importance of discrimination was 9 percent of the existing Anglo–Mexican American income difference.[29] Our evaluation of the methods employed for these two estimates suggests that the first overestimates discrimination against Chicanos and that the second study underestimates it.[30] But these evaluations, like the studies themselves, must be regarded cautiously since they are made from a human-capital framework which is not adequate for explaining variation in labor-market earnings.

TABLE 3.7. *Median income of Spanish-surname families as a percent of Anglo income, Southwest, 1959 and 1969*

	1959	1969
Southwest	65%	66%
Arizona	68	74
California	79	73
Colorado	67	69
New Mexico	57	67
Texas	52	58

Sources: U.S. Bureau of the Census, "Persons of Spanish Surname," *Census: 1970, Subject Reports*, PC(2)-1D, table 12, pp. 81–83. Idem, *Census: 1970, General Social and Economic Characteristics*, PC(1)-C4, *Arizona*, table 57, pp. 109–110; PC(1)-C6, *California*, table 57, pp. 403–404; PC(1)-C7, *Colorado*, table 57, pp. 158–159; PC(1)-C33, *New Mexico*, table 57, pp. 134–135; and PC(1)-C45, *Texas*, table 57, pp. 451–452.

Changes over Time

Whether the incomes of the Chicano population are increasing as rapidly as those of the rest of the population is almost as important a question as the current income position of this group. Given an income gap, the number of years required to eliminate this gap obviously depends upon the rates of change of Chicano and Anglo incomes. Table 3.7 presents the picture in terms of family income for the ten years 1959–1969.

Chicano family income relative to Anglos in the Southwest stayed approximately the same during the 1960's. Relative gains for Chicanos in Arizona, New Mexico, and Texas were offset by a decline in California.

Changes in male and female relative incomes are shown in table 3.8. For males slight gains were recorded in the Southwest as a whole, larger gains were made within most states of the region, and relative income fell slightly in California. Female Mexican Americans in the Southwest experienced some gain in relative income over the decade.

The overall impression provided by these statistics is that the relative income of Chicanos is improving throughout the Southwest except in California. The result has been a marked convergence among the southwestern states in the relative income experience of Chicanos over the last ten years. None of our income statistics show improvement for California's Chicano population, and the family income figures show a definite decline. Since Mexican Americans have long enjoyed their best comparative income experience in California, their lack of gains in that state during the 1960's prevents any optimism about the rapid attainment of equality of Mexican American income with that of Anglos.

There are two possible explanations for the absence of income gains in California. One is that, although Chicanos in that state have penetrated the job structure through craft and clerical positions (see chapter 4), they are now unable to move into the high-paying managerial and professional sectors because of discrimination and educational deficiencies. The second is that the high absolute and relative incomes in California have attracted large numbers of less-qualified Chicanos from other parts of the Southwest (especially Texas) and from Mexico (through legal and illegal immigration), who must start at the bottom of the job structure. The competitive disadvantages in the labor market of these migrants hold down the average incomes of the entire Mexican American population, even though some in the group are penetrating the high-wage job sectors. No doubt, both explanations contain some degree of truth.

It should be noted that the migration of Chicanos to California between 1960 and 1970 aided their income experience, when the Southwest as a whole is examined. The fraction of the Southwest's Spanish-surname population which lived in Califor-

TABLE 3.8. *Median income of Spanish-surname males relative to Anglos and females relative to all whites, Southwest, 1959 and 1969*

	Males, 25–64: % of Anglo		Females, 14 and over: % of all whites*	
	1959	1969	1959	1969
Southwest	63	66	67	76
Arizona	65	75		77
California	74	72	85	84
Colorado	69	72	76	79
New Mexico	58	64		80
Texas	51	58		73

Sources: U.S. Bureau of the Census, "Persons of Spanish Surname," *Census: 1970, Subject Reports*, PC(2)-1D, table 9, pp. 42–59; and "Negro Population," PC(2)-1B, table 8, pp. 90–129. Idem, *Census: 1970, Detailed Characteristics*, PC(1)-D4, *Arizona*, table 193, pp. 578–582; PC(1)-D6, *California*, table 193, pp. 2263–2276; PC(1)-D7, *Colorado*, table 193, pp. 623–626; PC(1)-D33, *New Mexico*, table 193, pp. 515–518; and PC(1)-D45, *Texas*, table 193, pp. 2087–2097. Idem, *Census: 1960*, vol. 1, *Characteristics of the Population*, pt. 4, *Arizona*, table 134, pp. 353–355; pt. 6, *California*, table 134, pp. 353–355; pt. 7, *Colorado*, table 134, pp. 295–296; pt. 33, *New Mexico*, table 134, pp. 279–280; and pt. 45, *Texas*, table 134, pp. 1062–1067.

*Includes almost all Spanish-surname females.

nia rose from two-fifths to one-half in that decade. Since personal incomes are larger in California than in the other states of the region, the effect of this population shift was favorable for Chicano incomes, assuming that the decline which occurred in their *relative* income in California was not totally offsetting.

4. The Job Market

Introduction

The settlement and development of the southwestern states during the latter part of the nineteenth century brought forth the discovery that Mexican Americans already living in the area and Mexican nationals who could be induced to travel north were a valuable source of cheap labor. Burgeoning industries which required large quantities of cheap, unskilled labor—especially farming, mining, and railroads—quickly exploited these sources. Although the wages they offered were low and the work hard, the response to recruiting efforts was substantial since those recruited had very poor alternatives to the jobs offered them.

Most employment of Chicanos (and Mexican nationals) well into the twentieth century was in Texas, Arizona, and New Mexico. Statistics on the foreign-born population of these states show that in 1900 about half of all foreign-born Mexican workers were employed in agriculture. The largest *shares* of employment held by this population, however, were in railroads and mining, where they comprised majorities of all workers. Much of the railroad employment was in construction—building road beds and laying tracks. Other occupations which employed many Mexican immigrants (from 10 to 25 percent of total employment) were domestic servants, waiters and waitresses, carpenters, laundresses, and retail-trade employees.[1] These humble beginnings demonstrated the capacity of Mexican-origin workers for hard physical work and led to their employment as unskilled laborers in irrigation development, the sorting and packing of fruits and vegetables, the canning and packing of food, and construction generally.[2]

Railroad construction and maintenance, particularly, relied upon cheap Mexican labor. According to one historian, "Most of the Mexican laborers who entered the United States in the first two decades of the century may have worked on them."[3] Carey McWilliams estimated that Mexicans made up 70 percent of the section crews on the large western railroads between 1880 and 1930.[4] In the latter year, the Santa Fe employed 14,000 Mexicans; the Rock Island, 3,000; the Great Northern, 1,500; and the Southern Pacific, 10,000. Most of these workers were probably supplied by labor recruiters in Texas from the vast number who immigrated legally and illegally across the Texas border.

Mexican immigrants during the 1920's partially replaced the European labor supply to American industry, which had been greatly reduced by immigration restrictions and World War I. Official Mexican immigration in this decade ran to almost half a million from 175,000 in the prior ten years.[5] The twenties saw Mexican American workers recruited for a number of northern manufacturing industries as well as for agriculture and the railroads. They appeared in significant numbers in Chicago—steel and meat packing; Detroit—automobiles; Ohio and Pennsylvania—steel; and Kansas City—meat packing.[6]

By 1930, Chicano males were still predominantly laborers—35 percent on farms and 28 percent in nonfarm work.[7] Only 7 percent were employed in white-collar jobs. Since then (more accurately, since the Great Depression), this minority population has been shifting from unskilled occupations to semiskilled and skilled manual jobs—and, during the 1960's, to white-collar positions. But up to and including the present, their occupation patterns have been and are very different from those of the majority population.

Occupations

Table 4.1 gives the 1970 occupational distributions for Chicanos, Anglos, and Negroes in the Southwest. Chicano males relative to their Anglo counterparts are overrepresented as farm and nonfarm laborers, service workers, and semiskilled workers (operatives). They are underrepresented as professionals, managers, and sales workers and are employed about as frequently as Anglos in clerical and craft jobs. The Chicano and Negro distributions are rather similar, although the former are more likely to be employed as craftsmen and less likely to be employed as service workers and laborers. Also, few blacks in the Southwest hold farm jobs, while 8 percent of Chicano male employment is still in farm work.

TABLE 4.1. *Spanish-surname, Anglo, and Negro
employment by occupation, Southwest, 1970*
(% employment)

Occupation	Spanish surname	Anglo	Negro
Male			
Professional	6.4	18.7	6.9
Managers	5.2	14.0	3.5
Sales	3.9	9.1	2.5
Clerical	6.6	7.2	8.7
Crafts	20.8	21.1	15.7
Operative	25.4	14.4	26.2
Service	10.5	7.1	17.6
Laborer	12.1	4.7	15.9
Farmers	0.9	2.1	0.4
Farm labor	8.1	1.4	2.4
Total	99.9	99.8	99.8
Female			
Professional	7.6	18.4	11.9
Managers	2.4	5.1	1.7
Sales	6.1	8.8	2.9
Clerical	27.9	40.3	21.7
Operative	23.3	7.6	12.2
Private household	5.4	1.9	17.4
Service	20.6	14.7	28.0
Other	6.7	3.2	4.2
Total	100.0	100.0	100.0

Sources: U.S. Bureau of the Census, "Persons of Spanish
Surname," *Census: 1970, Subject Reports*, PC(2)-1D, table 10,
pp. 60–77. Idem, *Census: 1970, Detailed Characteristics*,
PC(1)-D1, *U.S. Summary*, table 224, pp. 746–748.

By weighting the percentages of a group employed in the occupations shown in table 4.1 with the median annual earnings of all persons for each occupation, we can obtain an index which summarizes the occupational position of a group. When we did this for California and Texas males (1970), the following results were obtained:

Ratios of occupational indexes:
Spanish surname to Anglo and Negro

	SS/A	SS/N
California	.85	.98
Texas	.81	1.07

Chicanos have an occupational position which is inferior to that of Anglos but is better than that of blacks in Texas. Their standing relative to Anglos is better in California than Texas, but this is due largely to a structure of occupational earnings which is more compressed (less variance) in Texas, rather than to actual distributional differences.[8]

Among females, Mexican Americans as well as Anglos find jobs most frequently as clerical workers, but Chicanas are three times more likely to work as semiskilled operatives. Anglo women are employed much more frequently in nonclerical white-collar positions than Chicanas. The major Chicana-black difference among women is that 45 percent of the blacks are in service (including private household) work compared to 26 percent of Mexican Americans.

Occupational Earnings

Table 4.2 compares the earnings of Chicanos in various occupations with the earnings of Anglos and Negroes. Data availability required the use of the Spanish-language–Spanish-surname population for the calculations. Consequently, the ratios in table 4.2 are biased upward compared to those which would be obtained if appropriate data were available for the Spanish-surname population (see the Introduction).

It is instructive to note initially that the Chicano-Anglo earnings difference is much larger for the all-occupational total than for any of the component occupations. This demonstrates the

TABLE 4.2. *Ratio of median earnings by occupation: Spanish language–Spanish surname to Anglo and Negro, 1969*

| | California | | Texas | |
	SLSS/A	SLSS/N	SLSS/A	SLSS/N
	Male			
Professional and technical	.86	1.20	.75	1.12
Managers	.85	1.25	.70	1.22
Sales	.86	1.31	.66	1.17
Clerical	.92	1.03	.75	.96
Craftsmen	.88	1.11	.70	1.06
Operatives	.88	1.00	.69	.85
Service	.91	.96	.72	.96
Laborers	1.08	.94	.95	.86
Farmers	.88	1.82	.70	2.08
Farm laborers	.88	1.38	.85	1.27
All occupations	.74	1.06	.59	1.02
	Female			
Professional and technical	.82	.87	.82	.83
Managers	.88	.89	.82	1.29
Sales	.91	.92	.93	1.08
Clerical	.89	.95	.80	1.10
Operatives	.87	.92	.80	.89
Service	1.02	.79	.92	.87
All occupations	.80	.90	.69	1.15

Sources: U.S. Bureau of the Census, *Census: 1970, Detailed Characteristics,* PC(1)-D6, *California,* tables 175, 176, pp. 1773–1874; and PC(1)-D45, *Texas,* tables 175, 176, pp. 1740–1811.

effects that the heavy concentration of Chicanos in the lower-paid occupations has on the earnings of the total group when they are compared to Anglo earnings. But even if Mexican Americans were somehow to match the Anglo occupational distribution, the ratios in table 4.2 indicate that their earnings would still be well below those of Anglos unless improvement *within* each of the occupational categories also occurred.

Chicano males earn less than Anglo males in all occupations except that of laborer (this exception will be discussed below). In contrast, Chicano earnings are better than those of Negroes in almost all occupations—substantially better in the white-collar categories and in farming.

Among females, the most interesting fact is that, in California, Mexican Americans earn less than blacks in all major occupations. This does not result from especially low earnings by the former—their earnings relative to Anglo women are similar to the relative earnings of Mexican American males—but, rather, occurs because of the high earnings of black females in California. Black females in that state now earn nearly as much as Anglo women in some occupations.

The earnings differences reflected in table 4.2 can be divided into two parts: (1) those caused by the fact of Chicanos holding the lower-paying jobs within each of the broad occupational categories, and (2) those due to the lower pay received by Chicanos when they are employed in the same job classification (but not in the same firm) as Anglos. The second factor is the much more important contributor to the low occupational earnings of this group. Evidence to this effect is presented below.

The occupational earnings of Chicanos compared to Anglos are much better in California than in Texas. The major factors involved in these interstate differences are the concentration of Texas Chicanos in South Texas, where wages are generally low; better labor-market qualifications of Chicanos in California (especially relative educational attainments); and, it seems likely, greater occupational discrimination in Texas. However, the occupational distributions (relative to Anglos) of Chicanos in California and Texas are approximately the same over the broad categories given in table 4.2. Therefore, if occupational discrimination is greater in Texas, it must occur in hiring for detailed occupations, for example, in the distribution of Chicanos among the specific craft, clerical, and professional jobs.

Industries

Little is unique about the broad industry attachments of the Mexican American work force, with the exception of continued disproportionate employment in agriculture. The fraction of this group employed in agriculture is two and one-half times the Anglo fraction. Even so, only 8 percent of Mexican American employment is now in this industry.

In addition to agriculture, Chicanos provide a large part of the labor supply to some of the nondurable manufacturing industries. For example, they were almost half of the thirty-four thousand female employees who worked in Los Angeles's apparel and textiles industry in 1970. Other nondurable sectors employing sizable fractions of Chicanos include food, leather products, rubber products, and cosmetic manufacturing.

Chicanos tend to be employed rather infrequently by governmental jurisdictions, although this generalization is subject to much area variation. In California less than 6 percent of government employees in 1970 were Chicano, compared to over 9 percent of all employment. In Texas, on the other hand, more than 15 percent of government employment was held by Chicanos, compared to 11.5 percent of all employment.[9] Much of the government employment of this group in Texas is in federal agencies located in South Texas, where Chicanos are a large part of the labor force. Traditionally, Chicanos are thought to be underrepresented in the public sector because of language problems, apprehension about dealing with government, and citizenship requirements of governmental agencies. However, active recruiting by public jurisdictions can overcome these barriers as was shown by the operation of the Emergency Employment Act (1971) in Los Angeles. One-fourth of the participants in that program were Chicanos.[10]

Labor-Market Processes

JOB-ALLOCATION THEORY

The process by which Chicanos come to hold inferior jobs is best explained by the "queuing" theory of worker allocation. In the queuing process each prospective worker gets in line (figuratively) for the highest-paying and otherwise most desirable job that he or she has a reasonable chance of acquiring. Employers move down the queue selecting those people who they think will perform best. Workers not chosen for the most desirable jobs must then get in line for the lower-paying and less desirable ones until they are selected for employment.

By the nature of this process, employers who pay high wages can usually choose from an ample (excess) supply of applicants. The employer's selection problem for such jobs then becomes one of reducing the number of applicants to a manageable size. The most efficient (i.e., cheapest) way of doing this for many employers has come to be the use of schooling credentials. These employers exclude from hiring consideration all workers in the queue who do not have the specified amount or kind of schooling. Other workers will not be chosen for high-wage jobs because they lack the requisite skills or attributes, and still others may be excluded on the basis of such factors as sex, race, or religion.

This queuing process distributes workers both among employers and among the various occupations. In most cases, workers first join the queues for the occupations they are interested in and qualified for, moving from high-wage firms to low-wage ones until they obtain employment in the occupation. If they are unable to find a job in their preferred occupation, they will line up in the queues for other, less desirable occupations. Some workers, particularly those who are not highly skilled, will quickly give up searching for employment in their preferred occupation in order to obtain any job with a high-wage firm. In such cases, the job security, advancement prospects, and other inducements offered by the high-wage firm are chosen over employment in the preferred occupation in a lower-wage firm.

In general, Chicanos are at a disadvantage in the queuing process because (1) their schooling and technical skills are low, (2) some lack facility with the English language and familiarity with labor markets, and (3) some employers discriminate against them. The result of these disadvantages, together with the queuing allocation process, is the allocation of this group, in numbers out of proportion to their population and qualifications, first, to low-wage employers and, second, to the less desirable occupations in high-wage firms.

Verification and a more complete understanding of this hypothesized allocation of Chicano workers is necessary if a policy for improving the outcomes of labor-market processes is to be devised. Unfortunately, little analysis of the problem has been done.

RESEARCH

David Taylor, in a study largely devoted to discrimination against nonwhites, reported on discrimination against Mexican Americans and Puerto Ricans (combined) in the Chicago "material handler" occupation.[11] After controlling the influence of a number of personal characteristics, he found discrimination of 15 cents an hour against Spanish-origin persons (compared to 31 cents an hour against nonwhites). When a regression was run which controlled for establishment as well as personal variables, the discrimination coefficient declined slightly to 13 cents an hour. These results are not consistent with the view that Chicanos are disproportionately allocated to low-wage firms (as was the case with nonwhites). Instead, they suggest the second kind of discrimination referred to above—allocation of Chicanos to inferior occupations in high-wage firms. This research, however, covered only twenty Spanish-origin workers and is, obviously, of limited value for that reason.

Research on industry allocations is more supportive of the queue theory. Fogel found a negative relationship between the average earnings of Anglos in an industry and the proportion of the industry's work force which is Chicano.[12] This relationship existed for four occupations—clerical, craft, foremen, and operatives—across seventeen industries (the all-occupation average wage for Anglos was the independent variable in each regression). Coefficients of determination ranged between .25 and .50. Of course, the fact that Chicanos are most frequently found in low-wage industries does not get at their allocation among establishments within given industries.

It is interesting to note that, in the cited study, Chicanos were infrequently employed in the communication and utilities industry. This may be related to the "regulated monopoly" nature of the industry, in which minimum profits are virtually assured so that there is little incentive to minimize labor cost, or it may be due to conservative management characteristics.

The proportion of laborers and service workers who were Mexican American was found to be unrelated to industry earnings levels in this research. This suggests either or both of the following: that members of this ethnic group who work in service and laborer occupations are well qualified compared to their Anglo competition and that there is little discrimination against Chicanos in these occupations.

The negative relationship between Chicano employment and wage rates has been clearly established across the various jobs (detailed occupations) encompassed by broad occupational categories.[13] The relationship appears to be strongest in the craft group (among manual occupations) and is nonexistent among laborers, confirming the findings of the previously cited industry analysis. When job schooling requirements (derived from the *Dictionary of Occupational Titles*) as well as occupational wage rates were used for the craft regression, the former had no explanatory power. This suggests that it is not the high educational requirements of manual jobs, by themselves, which produce the least desirable jobs for Chicanos but rather the queuing process, which permits employers to hire workers for high-wage jobs on the basis of educational qualifications and ethnicity.

Fred H. Schmidt's study of 1967 Equal Employment Opportunity Commission data tends to support the queuing theory.[14] He found that Chicanos were less frequently employed in firms with "prime" government contracts than in other firms despite the existence of nondiscrimination clauses in all federal government contracts and the efforts of the Office of Federal Contract Compliance (OFCC) to enforce these clauses. As noted by the author, this finding probably means that "prime" contractors are also high-wage firms which can be selective in employee hiring. Their selectivity has tended to exclude Chicanos, either discriminatorily or on a qualification basis. OFCC and EEOC enforcement efforts may be changing prime contractor hiring practices, but if such practices have a long history, discernible change will be slow.

Based upon these and other findings the following summary conclusions by Fogel appear to be justified:

In the queuing process which implicitly takes place in labor markets, workers line up for the high wage (and otherwise desirable) jobs. Because the supplies of labor for these high wage jobs are ample, the selection of employees can and does put great emphasis on worker qualifications, especially formal education, and, at times, on discrimination for reasons of race, nationality, sex, etc. Few Mexican Americans are selected for the high wage jobs because they tend to have low educational attainments and because, at times, they are discriminated against. Mexican Americans, therefore, must get in line for low wage jobs. They are selected with relative frequency for these jobs because they comprise larger proportions of labor supplies for them, and because their qualifications, compared to those of non-Mexican American workers with whom they compete for low wages, are better, many of the more educated workers having already taken high wage jobs.[15]

This general explanation is consistent with the comparatively poor earnings and employment experience of Chicanos in the better-paid occupations and their comparatively good experience in laborer occupations. It is also consistent with the general improvement of Chicano labor-market experience observed in World War II and the late 1960's.

OTHER JOB-ALLOCATION RESEARCH

In California, Chicanos in each broad occupational category, except the services, are distributed over the jobs within the category in roughly the same way as are Anglos; in other words, although Chicanos tend not to be employed in the best of the job classifications they are not *greatly* concentrated in the worst of the classifications either. (This is reflected in the high ratios on the right-hand side of table 4.3.) The situation is different in Texas, however, where the job distributions of Mexican Americans and Anglos do differ significantly, to the adversity of the former.

Contrastingly, in both California and Texas, the *earnings* of Chicanos in each broad occupation except that of laborer are well below the earnings of Anglos (the first two columns of figures in table 4.3). The unweighted average of Chicano-Anglo earnings ratios for nine major occupational categories was .84 in California and .65 in Texas (1959 data).

The findings, put together, indicate that the low earnings of Chicanos within each broad occupation are largely associated with labor-market processes which allocate members of this

TABLE 4.3. *Ratio of average earnings and job indexes by occupation, Spanish surname to Anglo, males, 1959*

Occupation	Earnings ratios		Job index ratios*	
	Calif.	Texas	Calif.	Texas
Professional	.84	.60	.95	.91
Managers	.80	.59	.97	.93
Clerical	.89	.71		
Sales	.83	.53	.94	.87
Crafts	.89	.64	.98	.91
Operative	.88	.58	.99	.88
Services	.81	.62	.87	.83
Laborers	1.03	.83	1.03	.99
Farm labor	.62	.73		

Source: Walter Fogel, *Mexican-Americans in Southwest Labor Markets*, pp. 122, 146.

*Indexes computed from median earnings for each detailed occupation within the major occupations, weighted by the proportions of the group (Chicano or Anglo) in the detailed occupations.

group to areas, industries, and establishments which pay low wages. Allocation to low-paying jobs within the major occupational groups obviously contributes to the low earnings, but once Chicano workers gain entry to a major occupation, it is employment in low-wage establishments which hurts their earnings most—lower pay than that received by Anglos who are doing similar work in better-paying firms.

The policy implication of this is that providing Chicanos with the requisite schooling and skills for entry to a major occupation grouping is not enough. Individual establishments, including those paying high wages, must become willing to make hiring and promotion decisions which do not discriminate against Chicanos.

The fact that Chicano relative job positions (as shown in table 4.3) are lower in Texas than in California suggests a hypothesis about discrimination against this group: discrimination declines in a stepwise fashion, first, permitting entry to an occupation (as appears to be the case for Chicanos in California), and, second, bringing about equitable allocation among low- and high-wage firms which employ workers in that occupation.

A 1967 study of employer reports to the Equal Employment Opportunity Commission emphasized the concentration of Chicanos in blue-collar occupations and their relative absence in the white-collar sector.[16] A "social caste" system which "endeavors to sustain a wall between blue and white collar jobs" was proffered as a possible explanation. Chicanos appear to be less successful in penetrating the white-collar sector where they are a relatively large proportion of the local labor force, suggesting that the forms of caste become more rigidly guarded in such cases. Other explanations are also tenable, however. For example, a relatively large sized Chicano population may be brought about by job opportunities in farm labor and other low-wage occupations. Then, failure to penetrate the white-collar sector would be due to the relative absence of white-collar skills in the Chicano work force. Similarly, a very recent study suggested that a high rate of migration by Chicanos to a local labor market has an adverse impact on their occupational status.[17]

Influences on Job Earnings

There is a tendency for Mexican American earnings relative to Anglos to be fairly high when the former are employed in jobs subject to a high degree of wage standardization in local labor markets.[18] Wage standardization refers to the degree of dispersion which exists about the average wage. It is usually small in the market presence of large organizations (public or private) and unions (but could also, theoretically, be very small with well functioning, competitive markets). Examples of jobs for which wage dispersion is small include mail carriers, public school teachers, plumbers, and longshoremen.

When Chicanos are employed in these jobs, their wages are relatively good—because most firms pay the standard wage or close to it. On the other hand, Chicanos are infrequently employed in such jobs. Job markets which are characterized by small amounts of wage variation seem also to be characterized by a set of rigid hiring requirements which Chicanos find hard to meet, for example, high school graduation and language competence. Civil service jobs are outstanding examples of the simultaneity of wage and hiring standardization.

The association between wage and hiring standardization apparently improves the relative earnings of Chicanos employed on these jobs but lessens their chances of obtaining such employment. Another impact is an increase in inequality of earnings among Chicanos (as well as other groups)—those who can get jobs in the "good" markets earn much more than those who cannot.

Changes over Time

There has been substantial improvement in the occupations held by Mexican American men over the last forty years (table 4.4). The gains were most rapid before 1950, presumably during World War II, and in the most recently completed decade, most likely between 1965 and 1970.

In the most recent period, Chicanos increased their proportion of employment in the white-collar occupations, especially the professional, managerial, and clerical groups. They also raised their employment in the craft groups, the best paid of the manual occupations. Occupations which experienced relative declines in Chicano employment were laborers and farm labor. The distributional shift was largely from these two occupations to the white-collar sector, although service employment also increased slightly.

These shifts in occupational distribution were larger than comparable shifts which occurred among Anglos. The result was a gain for Chicanos in relative occupational position between 1960 and 1970 as shown by table 4.5.

TABLE 4.4. *Occupational distributions of Mexican American men, Southwest, 1930–1970*

Occupation	1930	1950	1960	1970
Professional and technical	0.9%	2.2%	4.1%	6.4%
Managers	2.8	4.4	4.6	5.2
Sales	2.4	6.5	3.6	3.9
Clerical	1.0		4.8	6.6
Crafts	6.8	13.1	16.7	20.8
Operative	9.1	19.0	24.1	25.4
Service	4.0	6.3	7.5	10.5
Laborer	28.2	18.7	15.2	12.1
Farmers	9.8	5.1	2.4	0.9
Farm labor	35.1	24.7	16.8	8.1

Sources: 1930–1960, Walter Fogel, "Job Gains of Mexican-American Men," *Monthly Labor Review* 91, no. 10 (October 1968):23. 1970, U.S. Bureau of the Census, "Persons of Spanish Surname," *Census: 1970, Subject Reports*, PC(2)-1D.

The relative income gains of Mexican Americans during 1960–1970, discussed in the previous chapter, were somewhat less than might have been expected from the occupational gains shown here. It must be realized, however, that shifts from broadly defined manual occupations to broadly defined white-collar classifications do not always raise incomes since some white-collar jobs pay less than average wages. Also, these occupational shifts are brought about by youthful entrants to the

TABLE 4.5. *Occupational position indexes of Mexican American and Anglo men, 1930–1970*

| | California | | | Texas | | |
	Mexican American	Anglo	MA/A	Mexican American	Anglo	MA/A
1930	35.8	53.3	.67	23.8	34.7	.69
1950	43.3	56.3	.77	28.0	41.5	.69
1960	46.9	57.9	.81	33.0	43.9	.75
1970	50.5	59.4	.85	37.0	45.7	.81

Sources: Same as table 4.4. Occupational earnings (California and Texas) for 1959 were used as weights for the calculation of all indexes.

labor market who must begin near the bottom of the white-collar wage structures. White-collar wages rise rather sharply with age, and this suggests that the recent modest occupational improvements of Mexican Americans will have a favorable influence on their incomes in future years.

5. The Rural Economy

The rural economy of the southwestern United States has traditionally exerted a strong influence upon employment and income opportunities for Chicanos. By the 1970's, however, the vast majority of Chicanos were living and working in the urban sector of the economy. Yet despite the rapid urbanization of the Chicano population, it would be an error to conclude that the rural sector is no longer significant. The 1970 *Census* disclosed that 14 percent of the Chicano population of the Southwest resided in rural areas. With respect to workers, this census reported that 10 percent of the employed Chicano labor force lived and worked in the rural sector of the economy. In addition, 5 percent of the Chicano labor force living in urban areas was actually employed in the agricultural sector of the economy. This latter situation is especially characteristic of the thousands of Chicanos who are seasonal migratory farm workers; their home base is often urban but their work place is usually rural.

It is not possible to obtain income figures for all Chicanos who depend on the rural economy. The incomes of those Chicano families who live in rural areas are lower than those of urban families—$5,220 in 1969 compared to $7,390—but the number of the former are few so that the annual income of all Chicano families is just $300 less than the urban figure.[1] Yet, these statistics tell little about the welfare of all Chicanos who depend upon farm work for employment.

It is also worthy of note that the Southwest is characterized by vast arid land areas with sparse sources of water. Hence, the population of the region tends to cluster into scattered oasis communities. In numerous localities Chicanos dominate these human enclaves. The fact that many of these small cities and little towns number slightly more than the arbitrary definitions used by the U.S. Bureau of the Census and the U.S. Department of Labor to designate a rural area should not deceive one into a hasty dismissal of the consequence of rural developments to Chicano group well-being. For, as with all ethnic groups in the United States, it is those members who live in or are dependent upon the rural economy for whom living conditions are the most squalid, the opportunities of advancement the most limited, and the incidence of poverty the most pervasive.

General Background

The harsh weather, the rugged terrain, and the scarcity of water have led to extensive experimentation with and adaptation to the land by the successive waves of inhabitants who settled the area which has become the southwestern United States. Ultimately, the industrial base was composed most prominently of agriculture, ranching, railroading, and mining. During the late nineteenth and early twentieth centuries, all of these industries were extremely labor intensive. To meet the demand for a cheap labor supply, Chicanos and Mexican nationals were sought. These jobs were characteristically in remote locations away from established population centers, dead-end with little chance of occupational advancement, and seasonal and casual.

For the Chicanos who are dependent upon the rural economy for their livelihood, agriculture has assumed prominent importance. The major immigration from Mexico has occurred in the twentieth century. Most of these original immigrants came from a rural and agricultural heritage in Mexico. The thousands of annual illegal entrants still tend to follow this heritage. Knowing little English and having few technical skills to offer an urban labor market, they frequently gravitate into working in one of America's most exploitative industries.

Since the Southwest became part of the United States, the trend in the ownership of its land has been decidedly toward greater control by large business enterprises with immense financial power. This pattern has been exacerbated in recent years by the merger activities of conglomerate corporations to include agricultural ventures within their vast empires. Fewer but larger individual farm enterprises have been the result of the consolidation movement of these growth-oriented enterprises. For the Chicano farm workers, the meaning of this trend has been that it is "almost impossible to convert hard work into a stable base for gain."[2]

A reading of the economic indicators in the product markets of the rural Southwest reveals growing farm sizes, extensive

mechanization, and rising farm income for a few corporations
while labor-market indicators show extensive underemployment
and pervasive poverty. It is not surprising that the 1970 UCLA
Mexican American Study Project described the prevailing rural
relationships as constituting a "caste system."[3]

Specific Considerations

When the Treaty of Guadalupe Hidalgo was signed in 1848 and
the Gadsden Purchase of 1853 was accomplished, the vast land
area contained fewer than 100,000 people of Mexican citizenry.
The treaty gave these people the option of returning to Mexico
or becoming United States citizens. During the remainder of the
nineteenth century it is estimated that fewer than 30,000 Mexicans immigrated into these same territories.

The policy of the United States with respect to immigration
from Mexico has historically been tied to agricultural policy. In
this sense, it is fair to say that immigration policy toward Mexicans has not been a settlement process but, rather, a labor policy. The perpetual depression conditions with respect to low
wages, irregular employment, lack of unionization, and high
unemployment that characterize the border and rural labor
markets of the Southwest are not accidents. They are caused by
either purposefully harmful acts of public policy or the indiffer-
ence of the federal government to the enforcement of its enacted
policies in order to cater to the desires cf the powerful economic
interests of the region.[4]

Thus, the situation has developed whereby legal immigration
from Mexico is comparatively insignificant in comparison with
illegal entry as the dominant characteristic of labor supply over
the years. The border policies, in turn, have been closely related
to movement of seasonal workers (both Mexican and Chicano)
within the United States. Immigration policies have consistently
manifested an interest in Mexican workers but shown very little
concern for Mexican settlers as potential citizens. The power of
administered immigration, as well as its influences upon both
the territorial dispersion and the economic status of Chicanos,
remains a topic in need of extensive research. For immigration
policy has not operated in a vacuum. It has reflected short-run

domestic economic developments and shaped long-run labor-market patterns and racial attitudes throughout the Southwest.

To be specific, it was not until the twentieth century that the flow of legal and illegal immigrants from Mexico became numerically significant. Julian Samora and Jorge Bustamante have documented the Mexican immigration process.[5] They show that there have been three major historical causes for the mass movements of Mexicans to the southwestern United States: the rise of the regional industries of the Southwest with their corresponding demand for cheap labor; the enactment of the Chinese Exclusion Act and Gentlemen's Agreement with Japan, along with the decrease in the number of European immigrants due to World War I and the subsequent immigration limitations, which sharply curtailed the regional supply of other sources of cheap labor; and the internal developments within Mexico—especially the extreme violence of the Mexican revolutionary war period of 1910–1919—which forced thousands of Mexicans to flee for their lives.

Mexican workers were welcomed into the rural Southwest until the Great Depression. Then, in an effort to reduce welfare costs and to open job opportunities for Anglos, many Mexicans (as well as some native-born Mexican Americans) were forcibly repatriated to Mexico. Samora and Bustamante indicate, however, that the repatriation effort was not successful in obtaining its total objectives since illegal entry began in earnest during those years.

World War II brought a reversal from the policies of the 1930's. Large numbers of farm workers were again needed in the Southwest. But the flow of Mexicans did not immediately respond to the demand due to fear of the draft and the fact that the Mexican economy was flourishing. To overcome these factors, a written agreement was made between the governments of the United States and Mexico to provide a large supply of farm workers. Mexico, although initially hesitant, finally agreed to the proposal after it declared war against Germany, Italy, and Japan. The agreement was formally reached in August 1942. It created the "Mexican farm labor program"—better known as the bracero program (a term based on the Spanish word for arms brazos, which means literally "one who works with his arms"). Legalized by the United States as Public Law 45, it was con-

ceived originally as a wartime emergency program. Specific
guarantees on transportation, housing, and working conditions
as well as minimum-wage rates were spelled out in the agreement. Braceros were limited specifically to agricultural employment, and any bracero employed in another industry was
subject to immediate deportation. Ernesto Galarza has
documented the history of the program.[6] He shows that it was a
"bonanza" to the farm growers. When the original programs
ended on December 31, 1947, the growers lobbied for exten-
sions. Under informal annual agreements, the bracero program
continued until 1951, when the procedure was once more formalized by statute under Public Law 78 during the Korean
conflict. When the war ended, the program continued to
flourish until finally terminated by the United States in December 1964. At its height in 1956, the number of braceros
totaled 450,000 workers for the year.

Officially the braceros were not supposed to have an adverse
effect on domestic Mexican American workers. When the program was continued during the eras of peace (as opposed to
labor-shortage periods during World War II and the Korean
conflict), however, the bracero program contributed to the
worsening of economic conditions in the rural Southwest for
native Chicanos. The bracero program acted to suppress wages
below the levels that would have otherwise existed. The result
was that the farm labor market in the Southwest was removed
from the effects of competition with the nonagricultural industrial sector.[7] It is likely, therefore, that the bracero program was
a prime contributor to the mass movement of Mexicans to urban
areas that occurred between 1950 and 1964.

The termination of the bracero program was by no means the
end of the flow of Mexican nationals into southwestern farm
labor markets. Illegal entry (see chapter 1) has, since the mid-
1960's, assumed epidemic proportions. In 1974, for example,
710,000 illegal Mexican workers were caught and deported by
the U.S. Immigration and Naturalization Service (INS). This
number represented 90 percent of all aliens deported during the
year. There are, of course, no figures available for the number
who were not caught. The INS estimates that, for every illegal
entrant that is apprehended, there are at least five who escape
detection.[8]

Most illegals have few skills and a limited command of English. Consequently, rural rather than urban labor markets have been more accessible to them. Numerous studies have warned that rural and border labor markets of the Southwest are being flooded with these rightless workers.[9] The commissioner of the INS stated ominously in 1971 that the trend in the number of illegal entrants "will go upward" and that the situation "is growing progressively worse."[10] Unfortunately, the illegal alien question has traditionally been regarded as nothing more than a "regional problem" by the federal government despite the fact that the prevailing situation is a mockery to the nation's immigration statutes.[11]

In addition to the aforementioned, there is another example of institutional manipulation of the labor supply: the commuters. David S. North aptly stated in 1970 that "the commuter is this generation's bracero."[12] The commuters are people who often live in Mexico but frequently work in the United States. They may or may not be United States citizens. Until 1921, there were no numerical limitations on immigrants to the United States. By 1924, the National Origins Act, which established an official immigration policy, had been adopted. Although natives of the Western Hemisphere were excluded from the quotas imposed by the act, all people entering the United States were required to be classified as either immigrant or nonimmigrant. Immigrants were defined as all entrants except those designated as nonimmigrants who are visiting the country temporarily "for business or pleasure."

For a short interval, workers who lived in Mexico but commuted to jobs in the United States were classified as "temporary visitors" who were free to cross the border "for business." By arbitrary administrative decision by the INS in 1927, however, the status of these people was changed to "immigrants." Subsequently, in 1929, the U.S. Supreme Court upheld the INS action with the famous decision that "employment equals residence" (thereby neatly avoiding the permanent residency requirement of the immigration statutes).

The best known category of commuters is that of "green carders" (so named after the original color of the identification cards they carry). These card holders are legal immigrants and at their will can move and work anywhere within the United States. A

second group of commuters are called "white carders" (similarly
named for the color of their crossing cards). They are classified as
"legal visitors" who can stay within the country for up to 72
hours at a time within a radius of 25 miles of the border. Legally
speaking, the "white carders" are forbidden to be employed.
Yet, as the U.S. Commission on Civil Rights found in the course
of its 1968 hearings in San Antonio, numerous "white carders"
are employed and many "green carders" do not reside in the
United States.[13] Many of the commuters cross the border daily
to jobs in the United States. Other seasonal commuters find
employment in the expansive agricultural areas of the Southwest
for months on end. In any case, the result is the same: the
commuters fill job openings, depress working standards, and
retard unionization efforts that would otherwise improve
Chicano economic welfare.[14] Since the cost of living in Mexico is
much lower than that of the United States, the income of the
commuters goes much farther than it would if they had to live in
the United States on a year-round basis.

In 1952, the secretary of labor was empowered to block the
entry of immigrants from Mexico if their presence would en-
danger prevailing labor standards. The Immigration Act of 1965
significantly increased this power by requiring that immigrants
who are job seekers receive a labor certification. The certification must attest to the fact that a labor shortage exists in the
occupation for which the immigrant seeks employment and that
his presence will not adversely affect prevailing wages and working conditions. The certification is made only once—at the time
that the immigrant makes initial application for entry. The certification procedure, however, is fraught with loopholes. North
estimates that only one of every thirteen workers seeking to
become an immigrant is subject to the certification process.[15]

There are additional requirements for a person seeking a
permanent immigration visa (green card) besides a favorable
labor certification. Among these are a good-conduct statement
from the Mexican police, a birth certificate, a Mexican passport,
a medical examination, and a favorable interview with an American consular official who decides if the applicant is of good moral
caliber and is unlikely to become a public charge. Once the
green card is issued, the bearer may come and go across the
border as long as no absence from the United States exceeds a

year and the individual has not been unemployed for over six months.

Not all green carders are Mexicans. But many of the Mexican green carders are employed in agriculture. In 1974, there were 3.9 million green carders of all nationalities in the United States. Of this total, 882,606 (or 23 percent) were Mexicans. Although a regional breakdown of the location of these green carders by national origin is not available, it can confidently be stated that the vast majority of the Mexican green carders are located in the Southwest or in Mexico.

The INS does conduct periodic commuter counts of those green carders crossing the border on certain days. One of these counts in October 1974 revealed that 39 percent of the commuting green carders were employed in agriculture.[16] Estimates of the number of green carders who cross the border *daily* to work in the United States have ranged from 50,000 to 70,000 people.[17] There are no approximations of the size of the work force who cross on a *seasonal* basis. Likewise, little is really known of the labor-market activities of the white carders. The INS reports that over 2.2 million white cards were issued in the Southwest between 1960 and 1969.[18] How many of these white carders actually abused their visiting privileges by seeking employment is unknown. Presently no date of crossing is stamped on the white card unless the crosser indicates an intention to go beyond a 25-mile radius of the border. Frequently, however, the border crosser does not state a desire to go beyond the 25-mile limit but, after crossing, simply mails the undated white card back to Mexico and proceeds to go wherever he or she wishes. If apprehended, the person simply states that he is an illegal alien and agrees not to contest his capture so as to obtain "a voluntary departure." After his return to Mexico at the expense of the United States government, his white card is ready for his arrival so that the entire process can be repeated. For this reason, Sheldon Greene, General Counsel of California Rural Legal Assistance, has correctly labeled the white-card procedure as constituting "a back door bracero program to benefit employers at the expense of the resident poor."[19]

The detrimental effects of the combined numbers of illegal entrants and commuters upon the economic opportunities for Chicanos cannot be overstated. Voluminous testimony and data

gathered in recent years by the U.S. Commission on Civil
Rights in 1968, by the U.S. Senate Subcommittee on Migratory
Labor of the Committee on Labor and Public Welfare (chaired
by Senator Walter F. Mondale) in 1969 and 1970, and by the
U.S. House of Representatives Subcommittee No. 1 (on illegal
aliens) of the Committee on the Judiciary (chaired by Con-
gressman Peter W. Rodino) in 1971 and 1972 provide ample
documentation of the deplorable state of affairs in the rural labor
markets of the Southwest.

Obviously not all illegal entrants and commuters are employed in the rural sector of the U.S. economy. Yet there is
some evidence that a substantial number of both categories seek
rural employment for at least part of each year.[20] The result is
that an already surplus rural population is expanded even more.
In fact, the pressure caused by the presence of these additional
sources of labor supply in some localities is a prime explanation
of why many Chicanos join the migratory farm labor force. It is
no accident of fate that thousands of commuters and illegal entrants find employment in South Texas—the very same geographical area from where over one-third of the nation's total
migratory farm workers (plus thousands of additional family
members) come. They are literally "pushed" into the migratory
stream by the seemingly endless source of alternative labor
supplies in their home area. Essentially, the history of federally
approved or condoned labor-supply policies in the Southwest
has served to guarantee to growers what amounts to a perfectly
elastic supply of labor at very low relative wage rates.[21]

With respect to migratory labor, the U.S. Senate Subcommittee on Migratory Labor conservatively estimates that about 40
percent of all Chicanos employed in agriculture are migrants.[22]
If allowance were made for illegal Mexican aliens, the percentages would undoubtedly be higher. The adversity that sur-
rounds migrant farm life has been recounted too often to bear
repeating. Suffice it to say, scarcely anyone becomes a migrant
farm worker if there are any other employment options available. The size of the migratory stream, estimated to be about
275,000 in the early 1970's, is contracting. The explanation rests
mainly with the rapid introduction of farm mechanization and of
new techniques. Most of these new methods have been devised
by federal support to agricultural research. One rural labor market expert testified before the Senate Subcommittee on Migra-

tory Labor in 1970: "I am simply saying that probably 95 percent of all the research moneys in the U.S. Department of Agriculture and its land-grant affiliates is technologically oriented, and, therefore, oriented toward the displacement of people."[23] Despite the trend toward fewer migrants, the Texas Good Neighbor Commission warned in 1971 that "those who think that soon there will be no migrant problem are simply deluding themselves."[24] Since the early 1960's, numerous governmental programs have been initiated to deal with the problems of migratory farm workers. Most, however, have dealt with health, housing, personal treatment, and education. Little attention has been given to occupational training for alternative nonagricultural (but not necessarily nonrural) occupations.[25]

The key factor that is often overlooked in efforts to encourage movement out of the migrant stream is that home-base conditions frequently force people to become migrants. As indicated earlier, until public policy efforts for migrant workers confront the commuter and illegal alien issues, it is doubtful that they can succeed. Mechanization may be reducing the demand for migrants, but there has been no comparable contraction in the forces that generate the supply. Previous manpower training programs for migrants have had little success in these migrant home bases. The explanation is essentially that the graduates of these programs find themselves forced into competition with the commuters, the illegal aliens, and the untrained local populace for the scarce number of job openings. Moreover, too often these job openings have wage rates that are lower than the training allowances provided by the manpower programs.

Several manpower programs have sought to provide services to migrants while they were in the process of migrating. In general, however, these migrant programs have encountered great difficulty in the "receiving" states which need migrants. These states are willing to provide seasonal employment opportunities, but they are often quite unwilling to encourage the migrants to settle permanently as citizens of their communities.[26]

Agricultural Labor Policy

It has been pointed out by Vernon Briggs's study of Chicanos in the rural economy that, although large farm owners of the

Southwest "are the most privileged group in American corporate society . . . the farmworkers survive only by the law of the jungle."[27] As most Chicanos who are employed in the rural economy of the Southwest are employed in agriculture, the prevailing public policies are as responsible as any other factor for the insufferable conditions under which many workers are employed.

The federal minimum wage was not extended to agricultural workers until 1966. By 1976, the agricultural minimum wage had reached a level of $2.00 an hour, $.30 an hour below the nonagricultural federal minimum wage. Even this low wage rate, which would not provide sufficient income to reach the federally established poverty threshold if it were possible to work full time year around (which it is not), is available only to workers employed by growers using more than five hundred man-days of farm labor in a single quarter. It is estimated, accordingly, that these meager provisions apply to only 13 percent of the agricultural farm workers. Agricultural workers are specifically exempt from the provisions of the Fair Labor Standards Act that require overtime pay for more than forty hours of work a week.

Social legislation for farm workers in the Southwest is notable for its virtual nonexistence. Prior to 1974, only one of the five states of the Southwest, California, provided unemployment coverage for agricultural workers. This vacuum was filled in December 1974 when the federal government moved to make these employees eligible nationwide for the first time. With respect to worker compensation, only California provided such coverage for job-related injuries or illnesses for farm workers. None of the states nor the federal government requires overtime payments for farm workers. Moreover, only California has a state minimum wage that exceeds the federal minimum wage for agricultural workers.

With respect to unionization, agricultural workers are excluded from the coverage of the National Labor Relations Act (NLRA). As a result, there is no legal requirement that any union be recognized as the appropriate bargaining unit. Moreover, there is no way to prevent unfair labor practices by either employers or unions. There have been repeated efforts to extend coverage of NLRA to farm workers, but they have always encountered strong grower opposition. Also, the support for such moves has been weak and at times divided in its goals.[28] The most notable effort to organize farm workers in the Southwest in recent history has been the drive of the United Farm Workers (UFW) under the leadership of César Chávez.[29] Chávez, however, does not seek simply an amendment to the NLRA that would extend coverage to agricultural workers. Rather, he has sought to have a period of pro-farm-labor legislation similar to the protection given to other forms of industrial unions when the original NLRA was passed in 1935, without the restrictive amendments later imposed by the Taft-Hartley Act (1947) and the Landrum-Griffin Act (1959).[30]

The lack of NLRA coverage is, of course, not the only obstacle that confronts efforts to establish unions for farm workers.[31] Organizational costs are high because work sites are scattered over vast geographical areas. Farm worker incomes are low, which makes it difficult to set dues high enough to cover these costs. Also, there are the large number of potential strikebreakers in the illegal aliens, commuters, and other underemployed local workers in the rural Southwest. The large numbers of migratory workers also represent an unknown factor with respect to their desire to affiliate with a permanent union. On the other hand, the rush toward consolidation of farms into fewer but larger units may eventually enhance the prospects of unionization in this sector of the industry.

On August 28, 1975, a new state law in California became effective that pertained specifically to its vast agricultural industry. Known as the California Agricultural Relations Act of 1975, its passage occurred as a result of several years of protests, picketing, boycotts, and violence over the issue of union recognition of farm workers. In particular, a jurisdictional controversy between the United Farm Workers and the International Brotherhood of Teamsters had escalated into a showdown of powers and antagonism. The new law established what was hoped to be an orderly procedure for selecting an exclusive bargaining agent through a supervised and secret balloting process. A special five-member Labor Relations Board was established to determine the appropriate bargaining units for elections and to hear unfair labor practice charges. The law specifies that an election petition can only be filed during a period in which the payroll of the particular agricultural enterprise includes at least 50 percent of the peak employment level of the previous year. This requirement is designed to recognize that the number of farm workers fluctuates widely over the course of a year. If an election were held outside the peak harvest season, many farm workers would be disenfranchised. Thus, the law requires that the election must be held within seven days of the actual filing of the petition. A union must have pledge cards from at least 50 percent of the workers in the prospective bargaining unit before an election can be ordered. For another union to appear on the same ballot, it must receive pledges from at least an additional 20 percent of the workers in the prospective unit.

Of particular consequence to United Farm Workers–Teamsters competition is a provision of the California law which provides for nullification of a collective bargaining contract which was in force on the date that the law took effect (August 28, 1975). This makes it possible for workers to select a new bargaining agent and negotiate a new contract without waiting for the expiration of the contract which governed their employment before the effective date of the new law. The nullification provision is a statutory resolution of the UFW contention that many of the Teamster-grower contracts signed in the last few years were imposed upon farm workers. Another important provision of the law substantially restricts the use of the consumer boycott by a union that loses an election.

During the first two months of the California law, the United Farm Workers won 114 elections (gaining bargaining rights for 12,750 farm workers), the Teamsters won 86 (involving 9,540 farm workers), and 13 elections resulted in a "no-union" vote (affecting 1,740 farm workers). In 36 cases, formerly Teamster contracts switched to the UFW while none reverted from UFW to the Teamsters. The law has not yet produced an orderly election process, however. Hundreds of charges have been filed with the Labor Relations Board protesting election procedures and the conduct of the growers and the two unions involved. Indeed, the Teamster–United Farm Workers rivalry is threatening the viability of the new law.

By February 1976, however, the expenses associated with the administration of the act (i.e., the conduct of the numerous certification elections and the processing of the numerous charges of unfair labor practices) had exhausted the budget of the Labor Relations Board for the entire fiscal year. Hence, the activities of the board were suspended from March 1976 until

July 1, 1976, when a legislative compromise was finally achieved and new funds were made available for the next fiscal year.

While the long-term impact of this landmark piece of legislation is yet to be determined, it does appear to be a step in the right direction—that is, toward resolving the issue of worker representation in California. Whether the law will be duplicated elsewhere by other states is also an open question.

Conclusions

It is true that employment patterns of Chicanos resemble those of Anglos and blacks with respect to the fact that the majority of each group reside and work in urban areas. Yet it is a source of serious error to conclude that the rural sector is no longer significant. To the contrary, employment in nonmetropolitan areas of the United States increased by 3.4 million people between 1960 and 1970. Moreover, it is reported by the 1970 *Census* that 49 percent of the poverty population of the nation is in the rural sector of the economy. Obviously, any serious effort to address national attention to the economically disadvantaged must include both the rural and the urban sectors of the economy.

As for Chicanos, the findings of lengthy Senate hearings in 1970 on conditions in the rural labor markets of the Southwest were summarized by Senator Walter Mondale, who observed: ". . . there are no effective restrictions on Mexicans coming across the border although the Department [of Justice] claims that there are. Working conditions are abominable and Mexican foreign commuters are often used to break strikes. There is either a wholesale violation of social and economic legislation or it does not extend to them. Their whole pattern of life and work is as bad today as it was 30 years ago."[32] Thus, the character of rural poverty in the Southwest is markedly different from that of other regions of the economy. For aside from their lack of coverage by the basic social legislation of the nation, Chicanos are faced with public policies that tolerate a continual flow of rightless workers with whom they must compete. In this sense, the plight of Chicano rural workers is an example of institutionally imposed and perpetuated poverty.

There is little to be gained by continuing to force rural workers and residents to move to urban barrios. Many rural Chicano

workers have severe language, educational, and skill deficiencies relative to the typical urban worker. Working conditions
could be made more humane by at least ending the second-class
citizenship status that excludes farm workers from all basic social
legislation. An extensive manpower program of investment in
the employment potential of these workers would assist them to
transfer to the jobs that are increasingly in the rural nonfarm
economy. Yet none of these reforms can hope to succeed until
the unfair and inequitable competition from Mexican nationals
and commuter workers is ended. Certainly these changes are
within the realm of the possible if they receive the national
public attention they deserve.

6. Public Policy Needs for Future Economic Opportunity

The economic inequality that has characterized Chicano life in the past has stemmed from a combination of diverse factors. Racial differences and cultural separateness have certainly been important explanations. These considerations, however, are probably less powerful explanatory factors than the historical situation under which the original Mexican population became citizens of the United States and the subsequent conditions by which the waves of later Mexican immigrants were introduced into the labor markets of the southwestern United States. The fact that the majority of these immigrants (and the illegal entrants as well) have come from impoverished rural backgrounds has made the adjustment process more difficult and perpetuated the stereotype images held by Anglos. As George I. Sánchez has vividly written, "Time and time again, just as we have been on the verge of cutting our bi-cultural problems to manageable proportions, uncontrolled mass migrations from Mexico have erased the gains and accentuated the cultural indigestion."[1]

Ideally, the United States has sought to become a homogeneous nation composed of heterogeneous groups. To this end, traditional public policy measures for human resource development (e.g., the Morrill Act of 1862, the open immigration policy until 1924, the Servicemen's Readjustment Act of 1944) have had a general population mandate. Yet, events of the post-World War II era have shown that, in many ways, the United States is a heterogeneous nation composed of homogeneous groups. The nation may conceive of itself as the "melting pot of the world," but it remains a fact of life that the melding of these different groups into a single population has never been fully realized.

The critical distinction as to who is assimilated and who is not is most vividly portrayed with respect to racial groups. Blacks, American Indians, Asian Americans, and Spanish-heritage Americans (especially those who are of mixed racial backgrounds) are disproportionately represented among the ranks of the economically disadvantaged. Grudgingly, but of necessity, public policy has come to recognize the need to develop selective programs that zero in on the needs of specific racial subgroups. The manpower programs of the 1960's represent a manifestation of this quest.

In the 1970's, however, the strategy of approaching social problems in terms of their impact upon subgroups came under political attack as being nationally divisive. Yet, it remains highly doubtful that public policies designed to enhance the earning power of individuals (i.e., manpower programs that focus on the qualitative dimensions of labor *supply* as opposed to fiscal and monetary policies that focus on the quantitative dimensions of labor *demand*) can function successfully under any other economic mandate. The really serious economic problems of the United States are unlikely to be found from a reading of aggregate averages. Such barometers often conceal more than they reveal.

The thesis that racial subgroups require special attention implies that there is a differential in the economic experience among the various subgroups that compose the American society. For Chicanos, the differences can be seen both in the labor-market statistics and in the experiences that Chicanos have had with various public policies that have neglected to address themselves to the specific problems that confront Chicanos in the labor market.

The Lack of National Attention

For a variety of reasons, the plight of Chicanos has been very slow to attract national awareness and concern. The geographical concentration of the vast majority of the Chicano population in five southwestern states is no doubt the principal factor. But even in the immense land area that is presently the Southwest, Chicanos have not been evenly dispersed throughout the region. Galarza has indicated that "there are minorities within minorities."[2] He contends that there are eight distinctly different regional groupings of Chicanos. They are the San Francisco Bay basin, metropolitan Los Angeles, the Central Valley of California, the Salt River valley of Arizona, the upper Rio Grande valley of New Mexico and Colorado, the Denver area, a

less defined (but principally southern and western) region of
Texas, and the "border belt."[3]

In addition to geographic considerations, it is also important
to keep in mind that it was not until well into the twentieth
century that vast numbers of Mexican immigrants came to the
United States. Sheer numbers are important to the ability of any
group to make known its presence. The Chicano population has
by the 1970's achieved sizable proportions. With an inordinately
high fertility rate, a tendency for large families, a continual flow
of legal immigrants, and a flood of illegal immigrants, it is not
surprising that the growth rate of the Chicano population is
accelerating in both absolute and relative terms.

To overcome the problems of group discrimination, it is essential to attract national attention. To do so, it has been necessary for Chicanos to press the federal government for recognition as a separate and distinct racial group. This effort has been
especially anguishing to the Chicano community, and, at times,
it has been divided over the issue. Reflecting the pressure of
racism in American society, many Mexican Americans desired to
cling to the designation of being "white." It was only after
Chicanos realized that many school districts in the Southwest in
the late 1960's were using Chicano students (who were considered "whites") to meet court-ordered racial balances to achieve
integration that a concerted effort was made for a separate racial
classification.[4] The issue came to a head in a school integration
suit in Corpus Christi, Texas, in 1970. In the subsequent ruling,
the U.S. district court held that Chicanos were a separate class
who were covered by the *Brown* vs. *Board of Education* (1954)
decision that forbade segregation of any group of children in
public school because of race, color, origin, or ethnic characteristics.[5] The decision was also of consequence because it made
clear that the relevant issue was discriminatory treatment—not
whether Chicanos were a majority or a minority of the school
district's population. The court observed that "when a group, as
a whole, is politically impotent and economically disadvantaged,
it invariably will find itself subordinated, in one respect or
another, to those who are politically and economically strong-
er."[6]

Subsequent court rulings and federal government compliance
directives have recognized Chicanos as a distinct racial grouping

for purposes of achieving integration. Likewise, the older and more conservative Chicano organizations have grudgingly joined with the more militant Chicano organizations in accepting the need for a separate racial classification.

Related to the group-identity issue has been the problem of gathering adequate labor-market statistics. In order to assess adequately both the present patterns and the trends over time, it is vital to have reliable statistics as a basis for an analysis of the degree and nature of the problem of discrimination. It is a comment on the lack of national interest in the status of Chicanos in the United States that only since 1950 have relatively reliable census statistics been available for this population grouping. It was not until 1970 that the U.S. Department of Labor began publishing statistics on its manpower programs with a "Spanish American" category (a term that is still quite unsatisfactory as it lumps Chicanos with Puerto Ricans, Cubans, and others from Latin America and Spain).

The Legacy of Unequal Treatment

As indicated in earlier chapters, discrimination against Chicanos has never been as formally overt as that against blacks and American Indians. Nonetheless, it has frequently taken informal manifestations that were very similar in results. McWilliams has noted the strange reluctance by the nation to consider the direct question of discrimination against Chicanos. He notes that the historical studies have almost exclusively spoken of "the Mexican problem," which he feels has focused public attention on the consequences rather than the causes.[7]

In discussing the long-run employment patterns in the Southwest, it is necessary to start with the industrial base imposed on the region since it became a part of the United States. McWilliams has shown that for the most part the historical tendency has been for Chicanos and Mexican nationals to be employed in work gangs, crews, or families. The large enterprises—the growers, ranchers, mine owners, railroad companies—were seldom concerned with these workers as individuals, only as groups.[8] Moreover, within these industries, workers of Mexican descent were not distributed across the broad array of available occupations. Rather, they were relegated to certain occupations which were heavily manual, dirty, seasonal, and dead-end with respect to advancement opportunities. Where unions existed, they too tended to exclude Chicanos from membership or, even if Chicanos were members, to establish work rules that effectively barred Chicanos from opportunities to compete with Anglo members for better jobs.[9] The craft unions in particular were closed to Mexican American workers.

The patterns, of course, became self-reinforcing over time. By hiring Chicanos and Mexican nationals in large numbers for certain types of jobs, they became stereotyped as being only good for certain kinds of work. The occupational patterns, in turn, determined the residential patterns. In the past, most of these jobs were in isolated rural areas. For those living in urban areas, their low economic status resulted in their living in their own camps or their own parts of town. The limited occupational horizon meant that there were scant opportunities to live elsewhere. Hence de facto housing and educational segregation patterns in the Southwest became as real as the de jure patterns for blacks in the Southeast. The means may have differed but the results were strikingly similar.

Since World War II, the Chicano population has rapidly urbanized. The industrial base of the Southwest has greatly diversified during this period. Yet, the legacy of the past denial of equal employment opportunity is not easily overcome. The stereotyped work attributes, together with the racism that is built into the institutions of society, have tended to replicate the past into the present. Chicanos, as discussed in earlier chapters, remain disproportionately concentrated in blue-collar occupations—especially in the laborer and operative classifications—and industries in which employment opportunities are declining, such as manufacturing, mining, and agriculture.[10]

Access to the occupations and industries that have the best chance for future growth is frequently unattainable for Chicanos. It is no longer overt barriers but, rather, the covert institutional practices that effectuate the discrimination process for many employers and unions. Education and its associated credentials have become a primary hurdle. With the possible exception of American Indians, no racial group in America has fewer high school and college graduates than do Chicanos. Although overt segregation against Chicanos was not required by statute in any

of the five southwestern states, it did occur as a matter of standard practice in both California and Texas.[11] The separation of
Anglo and Chicano students in Texas was reinforced by the
widespread practice of local school boards not enforcing the
compulsory school attendance for Chicanos.[12] In California, the
segregation policies were more subtle. School districts were ger-
rymandered, transfer policies allowed students to be shifted
from one school district to another, and, in some instances,
students from designated ethnic groups were required to attend
specified schools within the school district.[13] Thus, until the
mid-1940's, school segregation was the unwritten policy of
numerous local schools throughout the Southwest.[14]

In 1945, the segregation policies of several school districts in
Orange County, California, were legally challenged. The decision in the *Méndez et al.* vs. *Westminster School District* ruled
in favor of the Mexican American students and their parents,
and, when the decision was affirmed on appeal in 1947, segregation against Chicanos was specifically forbidden in California. A
similar case was filed in 1948 in Texas (*Delgado* vs. *The Bastrop
Independent School District*), and it too was won by the Chicano
plaintiffs. These two decisions were primarily responsible for
terminating the purposeful segregation practices against
Chicano students. The issue, however, has lingered in a number
of areas with a finding as late as 1970 in Corpus Christi, Texas,
that the local school district knowingly perpetuated a segregated
school system against both Chicanos and blacks.[15]

The problem of de facto segregation as well as unequal quality
of educational opportunity for Chicano students remains a real
issue in many parts of the Southwest. The U.S. Commission on
Civil Rights, as part of its Mexican American Education Study
conducted in 1970 and 1971, confirmed the fact that Chicanos
were significantly isolated in de facto segregated schools
throughout the region and that they severely suffered from "cultural exclusion" with respect to curriculum, textbooks, and in-
structional methods.[16] The commission recommended extensive
reliance upon bilingual education and the addition of course
material which related the Chicano heritage and contribution to
the cultural development of the region.

In addition to education, however, there are other institutional barriers that require public attention. Hearings held in
Houston, Texas, in 1970 by the U.S. Equal Employment Oppor-

tunity Commission (EEOC) afforded the first public occasion for the EEOC to learn of the effect of covert discrimination upon the spectrum of employment opportunities for Mexican Americans.[17] Testimony was given that numerous employers and unions in the past had purposely excluded Chicanos from employment except for the most menial tasks. These earlier patterns, however, were seen as being duplicated in the present by the fact that the typical method of hiring is by referrals from current workers. Accordingly, if there were no Chicanos employed in the past, it is virtually impossible for any to be hired in the future under these arrangements. In addition, repeated testimony by employers disclosed that the standard procedure for occupational advancement is via internal job promotion. The combination of internal referrals and internal promotion practices virtually assures that past employment patterns will be perpetuated into the future.

The EEOC also heard extensive testimony by employers that many use aptitude tests, high school diplomas, honorable military discharges, physical examinations, and no-arrest records as employment screening devices with little concern given as to whether these requirements have anything to do with job performance. If job requirements are not related to employee performance, absolutely no level of qualification for employment can be set that will result in a better labor force as determined by employee productivity and effectiveness. Without proper performance validation, the effect of these practices is to deny equal opportunity for Chicanos (and other excluded groups) to be considered for employment and promotion.

Many craft unions—especially the mechanical building trades (electricians, plumbers, sheet metal workers, iron workers, operating engineers, and elevator constructors)—have long histories of racial exclusion. Hence, it was not surprising for the EEOC to find few, if any, Chicanos in the membership of most of the Houston unions.[18] Traditionally, membership in the mechanical crafts has been restricted largely to relatives of members. As minority groups were usually denied entry to the membership in the mechanical crafts, obviously they could not have relatives who were members. Hence, this institutional practice of nepotism served to keep the racial composition of these unions the same over the years. During the mid-1960's, civil rights groups brought pressures on the federal government to open the admission procedures to all people on an equal basis.[19] The response has usually been the establishment of "objective standards" which closely resemble the credentials required by most large private employers (e.g., written examinations, high school diplomas, no-arrest records, and physical examinations). Thus, again the subtleties of the "cult of credentialism" have replaced the boldness of overt bigotry as the employment obstacle to overcome.

There is a need for a study that specifically examines Chicano experiences with craft and industrial unionism. The fragmentary evidence that is available does indicate that Chicanos have had experiences quite similar to those of blacks.[20] Industrial unions have been reasonably accessible as have been the nonmechanical, less skilled crafts. The EEOC hearings in Houston in 1970, however, disclosed that one of the largest industrial unions—the International Longshoremen's Association (AFL-CIO)—in that major port city still at that late date had three segregated local unions: one for Anglos, one for blacks, and one for Chicanos.[21] Moreover, in addition to membership segregation, testimony was given that the black and Chicano locals were assigned the task of loading and unloading the dirtier and more dangerous cargoes.

Because trade unionism has been of significant benefit to many Anglo workers, it is vital that Chicano workers also have equal access to all such organizations. Too often, when studying employment problems of minority groups, one tends to seek new solutions, when, in fact, older programs that have achieved substantial gains for Anglos are dismissed from serious thought. Unionism is a prime example.

The Required Public Responses

In the preceding pages, the present-day results of the heritage of unequal treatment have been documented. The employment and income experiences of Chicanos have been shown to be distinctly different from those of Anglos. As their plight has gradually won national recognition, the task of selection of the proper corrective policy mix has arisen. Obviously, Chicanos benefit, along with all other working people, from aggregate public policies that actively pursue the goal of full employment.

Tight labor markets facilitate changes in employment patterns. But the experience of the mid-1960's has shown that the fiscal and monetary policies (which are the mainstays of full-employment programs) are necessary but not sufficient conditions to meet the aspiring needs of racial and ethnic minorities. The "type of job" is often as important as the "quantity of jobs." Hence, since the 1960's, parallel policies dealing with manpower development and with antidiscrimination have been vital components of public policy intervention into the labor markets. Potentially, Chicanos should benefit from both of these policy thrusts. In addition, the question of border and immigration policies are of serious consequence to the improvement of collective Chicano welfare.

There is general agreement in the literature that labor-market discrimination does exist against Mexican Americans but that its effects are less severe in terms of depressed income and denial of employment opportunities than that confronting blacks. The generalization, of course, does not mean that all blacks are worse off than are all Chicanos. Rather, the research studies show that, on the average, the industrial penetration rates and the occupational positions of Chicanos are better than those of blacks. Moreover, the incomes of Chicanos are significantly higher than the incomes of blacks despite the fact that Chicano educational levels are considerably below those of blacks.[22] There is also some evidence that the earnings and incomes of Chicanos are raised more than those of blacks as a result of the completion of manpower training programs.[23] The implication of these findings is clear: a considerable payoff to Chicanos and to society can be gained by public efforts to develop the educational and job skills of Chicanos. Adequately trained Chicano workers are more able to overcome discriminatory job barriers than are other racial minorities.

The implication should not be drawn, however, that antidiscrimination measures are of less need for Chicanos. On the contrary, there is a desperate need in the Southwest to demonstrate to Chicano youth that it is possible to advance on the basis of the content of one's character and the skill that one possesses. The chronic school dropout problems of Chicanos can only be overcome if these youngsters can be assured that education and training will bear equitable returns for effort expended. For although it is true that Chicanos do better in economic terms than do blacks with equivalent educations, it is also a fact that Chicanos receive less in economic returns than do Anglos with comparable educational attainment.[24] This disparity not only denies opportunities but also stultifies aspirations and, thereby, reduces occupational horizons.

It is likely that Chicanos have benefited and will continue to benefit from the protections of the equal employment opportunity section (Title VII) of the Civil Rights Act of 1964. Aside from the moral declaration that discrimination is illegal, the act has provided a complaint procedure for aggrieved individuals. In 1972 the authority of the U.S. Equal Employment Opportunity Commission (EEOC) was increased so as to provide it with litigant powers, and its jurisdiction was expanded to include coverage of state and local governmental bodies and educational institutions. This expansion of EEOC authority should increase greatly the significance of Title VII protections to Chicanos. The activities of the EEOC are especially important to the two million Chicanos living in Texas since it is the only state in the Southwest that does not have any statutes or enforcing agencies to guarantee that fair employment practices will prevail within its boundaries.

It is also likely that Chicanos will benefit greatly from a concerted attack by governmental antidiscriminatory bodies upon institutional discriminatory practices. Overt discrimination appears to be less of a present problem for Chicanos than it is for blacks. But credential requirements are a primary explanation for the paucity of Mexican Americans in white-collar occupations, growth industries, and mechanical craft unions. To this end, the continuing efforts of the EEOC to have job credentials be demonstrably related to job requirements may prove to be of extreme importance to Chicanos.

As for the issue of cultural barriers that may be associated with adverse employment experiences for Chicanos, this issue does deserve a very high research priority. A number of federal manpower programs—Job Corps, the National Migrant Program, Manpower Development and Training Act (MDTA) institutional instruction—have been forced to make significant changes to adapt to the cultural characteristics of low-income Chicanos.[25] The program designs that were molded to meet the needs of Anglos and blacks did not prove to be transferable to Chicanos. Indeed, as discussed in chapter 2, a special federal program tailored to the needs of Chicanos, known as Operation SER (the acronym is the Spanish infinitive for the verb *to be*) has grown in size and scope throughout the Southwest since its inception in 1965 in Corpus Christi and Houston, Texas. A better understanding of the significance, if any, of cultural values to labor-market experience could contribute greatly to the design of the proper mix of human resource development and antidiscrimination measures that are needed to assure a climate of equal economic opportunity for all people.

And lastly, an assessment of the prospects for the future must mention again the massive problem area of continued illegal entry and commuting workers. Senator Walter Mondale described the prevailing situation along the U.S.-Mexican border as "a major hemorrhage."[26] That is an apt simile from the standpoint of the nation as a whole and, especially, that of the low-skilled workers of the Southwest. But the major effects of this "hemorrhage" are on the Chicano segment of the Southwest's population and on the credibility of public policy concern with Chicanos as an economically disadvantaged group.[27] It does not make sense to develop a policy with programs aimed at removing the disadvantaged status of the Chicano population while at the same time doing little or nothing to stem the flow of immigration which continually adds to this population workers who have low amounts of schooling and job skills and, therefore, must take low-status jobs at low wages. Juxtaposition of these two policies casts doubt on the seriousness with which the first is being pursued and suggests, instead, that the nation's concern with Chicanos as a disadvantaged group is not sufficiently strong to bring about the most effective remedy available to end that disadvantaged status—an end to uncontrolled immigration.

The choice confronting those interested in improving the economic status of Chicanos in the Southwest is clearcut. One possibility is to continue the present border situation whereby deterrence is minimal, punishment is scant, and law enforcement is limited. The result is and will continue to be a grudgingly slow pace of group economic improvement. The other alternative is to impose and to enforce strong restrictions upon illegal entrants and commuting workers, as well as upon employers who hire illegal workers.[28] It is very likely that the latter course can provide a climate for more rapid economic progress. With the high incidence of low-income families and of unskilled and semiskilled blue-collar workers that characterizes present Chicano economic patterns, it makes no sense to perpetuate what is tantamount today to being an open border through which additional supplies of competing workers can flow literally at will. A tight border policy must, therefore, be an essential component of any serious public policy strategy to improve Chicano economic welfare.

Notes

INTRODUCTION

1. Leo Grebler, Joan W. Moore, and Ralph C. Guzman, *The Mexican-American People*. Also referred to in the text as the report of the Mexican American Study Project of the University of California at Los Angeles.
2. These *Current Population Reports*, published by the U.S. Bureau of the Census, are prepared from monthly probability surveys of households. In 1973, the surveys began to provide monthly data on the Spanish-origin population. Previously, between 1969 and 1973, one survey each year provided statistics for this population.
3. This figure is an approximation because it was computed with the imprecise technique of algebraically using medians as though they were arithmetic means.
4. Respondents designated their own origin from a list provided for this purpose. Spanish-surname enumerations result from *Census* identifications, using 8,000 surnames. Spanish-language identifications come from a question on "mother tongue."

1. THE PEOPLE

1. Rodolfo Acuña, *Occupied America*, pp. 24–27.
2. Carey McWilliams, *North from Mexico*, p. 102.
3. Ibid., p. 98.
4. Ibid., p. 103.
5. U.S. Bureau of the Census, "Persons of Spanish Ancestry," *Census of Population: 1970, Supplementary Report*, PC (S1)-30, tables A and D, pp. 11, 111 (hereafter cited as *Census*).
6. *Los Angeles Times*, quoting Joseph Waksberg, associate director of the bureau, April 26, 1973.
7. Leobardo F. Estrada, José Hernández, and David Alvírez, "Using Census Data to Study the Spanish Heritage Population of the United States," pp. 7–8. See also *Confederación de La Raza Unida et al.* vs. *George H. Brown, Director of the U.S. Census et al.*, Northern District, California, Civil Action Number C–71–2285, 1973; and Public Advocates, Inc., "California's and

the Southwest's Largest Minority—One in Six a Chicano," San Francisco, January 1972. U.S. Bureau of the Census, "Persons of Spanish Origin in the United States: March 1973," *Current Population Reports*, P–20, no. 259.

8. U.S. Bureau of the Census, "Persons of Spanish Origin: March 1973," no. 264, pp. 7–9.

9. U.S. Bureau of the Census, "Fertility Variations by Ethnic Origin," *Current Population Reports*, P–20, no. 226, table 1, p. 3.

10. *Census: 1970, General Social and Economic Characteristics*, PC(1)–C1, *U.S. Summary*, table 85, p. 380.

11. U.S. Bureau of the Census, "Persons of Spanish Ancestry," table 1, p. 1.

12. Estrada, Hernández, and Alvírez, "Using Census Data to Study the Spanish Heritage Population," p .7.

13. Julian Samora, "Mexican Immigration," in *Mexican-Americans Tomorrow*, ed. Gus Tyler, pp. 60–80.

14. U.S. Department of Justice, Immigration and Naturalization Service, *Annual Report*, 1971, table 12A, p. 52.

15. Ibid., p. 43.

16. Ibid., p. 38.

17. Tim Bakerville, "The Border Game," *West Magazine, Los Angeles Times*, September 17, 1972.

18. *Los Angeles Times*, January 13, 1973.

19. Ibid., January 14, 1973.

20. Ibid., December 17, 1971, and November 9, 1972.

21. "Immigration: Revolving Door," *Newsweek Magazine*, July 23, 1973, p. 24.

22. Ibid.

23. *Los Angeles Times*, December 9, 1972.

24. U.S. Bureau of the Census, "Persons of Spanish Origin," *Census: 1970, Subject Reports*, PC(2)–1C, tables 1 and 4, pp. 1, 32–45.

25. Ibid.

26. Ibid.

27. U.S. Commission on Civil Rights, Mexican American Educational Series, *Study Report I, Study Report II, Study Report III*.

28. U.S. Commission on Civil Rights, *Study Report II*, p. 41.

29. Leo Grebler, Joan W. Moore, and Ralph C. Guzman, *The Mexican-American People*, p. 150.

30. *Census: 1970, General Social and Economic Characteristics*, PC(1)–C1, PC(1)–C4, PC(1)–C6, PC(1)–C7, PC(1)–C33, and PC(1)–C45; table 51 of each volume.

31. Ibid.

32. Fred E. Crossland, *Minority Access to College*, p. 15.

33. Anne M. Young, "The High School Class of 1972: More at Work, Fewer in College," *Monthly Labor Review* 96, no. 6 (June 1973): 26–32. It should be stressed that this is a national survey including persons of Spanish descent other than Chicanos of the Southwest.
34. U.S. Commission on Civil Rights, *Study Report III*, p. 48.
35. Noel Greenwood, "Five-Million-Dollar Bilingual Education Bill Signed," *Los Angeles Times*, December 21, 1972.
36. U.S. Bureau of the Census, "Persons of Spanish Origin in the United States: November 1969," *Current Population Reports*, P–20, no. 213, tables 10 and 13, pp. 14, 17.
37. Ibid., table 19, p. 25.
38. Jack D. Forbes, *Mexican-Americans*, p. 16.
39. Paul Horgan, *Great River*, vol. 1, *The Indians and Spain*, and vol. 2, *Mexico and the United States*.
40. Paul Bullock, "Employment Problems of the Mexican-American," in *Mexican Americans in the United States*, ed. John H. Burma, p. 149.
41. Ibid.
42. Henry M. Ramírez, "America's Spanish Speaking: A Profile," *Manpower*, September 1972, p. 33.
43. Grebler, Moore, and Guzman, *The Mexican-American People*, p. 10.
44. Ibid., chaps. 16 and 18.
45. Ibid., p. 439 (the emphasis is supplied).
46. U.S. Bureau of the Census, "Population Characteristics," *Current Population Reports*, P–20, no. 244, table B, p. 2.

2. LABOR SUPPLY

1. U.S. Department of Labor, *Manpower Report of the President*, 1973.
2. These and other labor-force participation rates that follow are from *Census: 1970*, unless otherwise noted.
3. *Census: 1970, Detailed Characteristics*, PC(1)-D1, *U.S. Summary*, table 203, pp. 640–648.
4. U.S. Department of Labor, *Manpower Report*, 1973, p. 98.
5. For these calculations only men from 25 to 64 years of age are considered. In the case of women, the age range considered is 25 to 59 years. Full-year work is defined as 50–52 weeks.
6. Gordon F. Bloom and Herbert R. Northrup, *Economics of Labor Relations*, 7th ed., p. 429.
7. U.S. Bureau of the Census, "Persons of Spanish Surname," *Census: 1970, Subject Reports*, PC(2)-1D, table 9, pp. 42–59; U.S.

Bureau of the Census, "Persons of Spanish Surname," *Census: 1960, Subject Reports*, PC(2)-1B, table 6, pp. 38–49.
8. U.S. Bureau of the Census, "Persons of Spanish Surname," PC(2)-1D, table 9, pp. 42–59.
9. From a special tabulation of ethnic enrollees data provided by the Financial and Management Information System of the Manpower Administration. The Public Service Careers, National On-the-Job Program, and Neighborhood Youth Corps Summer Program were not included in the tabulation.
10. U.S. Department of Labor, *Manpower Report*, 1973, p. 103.
11. Ibid., p. 115.
12. See Walter Fogel, "Summary Report VI: Los Angeles City and County," in *Emergency Employment Act: The PEP Generation*, ed. Sar Levitan and Robert Taggart, pp. 135–160.
13. Herbert Hammerman, "Minority Workers in Construction Referral Unions," *Monthly Labor Review* 95, no. 5 (May 1972): 17–26. Hammerman's data are from EEOC surveys providing information on "Spanish Americans," a category more inclusive than the one used elsewhere in this review. It is not possible to extract data for Chicanos in the Southwest, although he concludes that these data are largely for those areas of high Spanish American participation in the labor force, such as southwestern urban areas.
14. See reports prepared by the Center for Human Resource Research, Ohio State University, 1966–1971.
15. U.S. Bureau of the Census, *Employment Profiles of Selected Low-Income Areas*, PHC(3), vols. 13, 39, 42, 48, and 50.
16. Ibid., tables 28 and 29.
17. For similar conclusions with respect to young Chicano workers, see Paul Bullock, *Aspirations vs. Opportunity*, chap. 4.
18. A study by the U.S. Tariff Commission reached a different conclusion. It found that the Border Industrialization Program may preserve some U.S. employment in firms which would transfer their entire production abroad in the absence of the program (U.S. Tariff Commission, *Economic Factors Affecting the Use of Items 807.00 and 806.30 of the Tariff Schedules of the U.S.*).
19. "Clothing Workers Win Union Representation," *Los Angeles Times*, February 25, 1974.

3. INCOME AND EARNINGS

1. U.S. Bureau of the Census, "Selected Characteristics of Persons and Families of Mexican, Puerto Rican, and Other Spanish Origin:

March 1971," *Current Population Reports*, P-20, no. 224, table
3, p. 5.

2. *Census: 1970, General Social and Economic Characteristics*,
PC(1)-C1, *U.S. Summary*, table 135, p. 459; U.S. Bureau of the
Census, "Persons of Spanish Surname," *Census: 1970, Subject
Reports*, PC(2)-1D, table 12, pp. 81–83.

3. The median family income of the Spanish-language–Spanish-
surname population of the Southwest in 1969 was $7,480 (*Census: 1970, Detailed Characteristics*, PC(1)-D4, *Arizona*;
PC(1)-D6, *California*; PC(1)-D7, *Colorado*; PC(1)-D33, *New
Mexico*; PC(1)-D45, *Texas*; table 198 of each volume).

4. U.S. Bureau of the Census, "Selected Characteristics of Persons and
Families of Mexican, Puerto Rican, and Other Spanish Origin:
March 1971," no. 224, table 3, p. 5.

5. Ibid.

6. U.S. Department of Labor, *Manpower Report of the President*,
1973, p. 101.

7. U.S. Bureau of the Census, "Persons of Spanish Surname," PC(2)-
1D, table 12, p. 81.

8. U.S. Bureau of the Census, "Selected Characteristics of Persons and
Families of Mexican, Puerto Rican, and Other Spanish Origin:
March 1972," *Current Population Reports*, P-20, no. 238, table
9, p. 8.

9. U.S. Bureau of the Census, "Persons of Spanish Surname," PC(2)-
1D, table 12, pp. 81–83.

10. Walter Fogel, *Mexican-Americans in Southwest Labor Markets*, p.
40.

11. Ibid., p. 36.

12. U.S. Bureau of the Census, "Persons of Spanish Origin," *Census:
1970, Subject Reports*, PC(2)-1C, table 10, pp. 121–134.

13. Ibid., table 4, pp. 32–45. Our calculations assume that Chicano
migration from the South is almost entirely from Texas.

14. See N. D. Humphrey, "Employment Patterns of Mexicans in Detroit," *Monthly Labor Review* 61, no. 5 (November 1945): 913–
923; Julian Samora and Richard Lamana, *Mexican Americans in
a Midwest Metropolis*; and Paul S. Taylor, *Mexican Labor in the
United States*.

15. U.S. Bureau of the Census, "Persons of Spanish Surname," PC(2)-
1D, table 12, pp. 81–83.

16. Ibid.

17. Ibid.

18. Fogel, *Mexican-Americans in Southwest Labor Markets*,
p. 40.

19. Ibid.

20. For example, see U.S. Bureau of the Census, *Census: 1970, Detailed Characteristics*, PC(1)-D6, *California*, table 197, pp. 2304–2344.
21. Walter Fogel, "The Effect of Low Educational Attainment on Income: A Comparative Study of Selected Ethnic Groups," *Journal of Human Resources* 1, no. 2 (Fall 1966): 31.
22. James Coleman et al., *Equality of Educational Opportunity*, pp. 274–275.
23. Jonathan King, "Social Inequality and Labor Force Participation," Ph.D. dissertation, University of California at Los Angeles, 1973, pp. 129–135.
24. U.S. Bureau of the Census, "Persons of Spanish Surname," PC(2)-1D, table 2, pp. 3–6.
25. Leo Grebler, Joan W. Moore, and Ralph C. Guzman, *The Mexican-American People*, p. 107.
26. See Lamar B. Jones, "Mexican-American Labor Problems in Texas," Ph.D. dissertation, University of Texas at Austin, 1965, p. 49.
27. U.S. Bureau of Labor Statistics, *Area Wage Survey*, Bulletin 1725–67.
28. Dudley L. Posten, Jr., and David Alvírez, "On the Cost of Being a Mexican-American Worker," *Social Science Quarterly* 53, no. 4 (March 1973): 697–709.
29. J. Allen Williams, Jr., Peter G. Beeson, and David R. Johnson, "Some Factors Associated with Income among Mexican-Americans," *Social Science Quarterly* 53, no. 4 (March 1973): 710–715.
30. Our evaluations are based on assessment of the income-related variables which were and were not included in the estimating procedures.

4. THE JOB MARKET

1. Roden Fuller, "Occupations of the Mexican-Born Population in Texas, New Mexico, and Arizona, 1900–1920," *Journal of the American Statistical Association* 23, no. 161 (March 1928): 64–67.
2. Fred H. Schmidt, *Spanish Surnamed American Employment in the Southwest*, p. 8.
3. Joan Moore, *Mexican Americans*, p. 21.
4. Carey McWilliams, *North from Mexico*, p. 168.
5. Leo Grebler, Joan W. Moore, and Ralph C. Guzman, *The Mexican-American People*, p. 64.

6. Moore, *Mexican Americans*, p. 22.
7. Walter Fogel, "Job Gains of Mexican-American Men," *Monthly Labor Review* 91, no. 10 (October 1968): 23.
8. Walter Fogel, *Mexican-Americans in Southwest Labor Markets*, p. 40.
9. U.S. Bureau of the Census, *Census: 1970, Detailed Characteristics*, PC(1)-D6, *California*, table 184, pp. 2012–2020; PC(1)-D45, *Texas*, pp. 1899–1904. See also Alfred J. Hernández, "Civil Service and the Mexican American," in *The Mexican American*, by the Inter-Agency Committee on Mexican American Affairs, pp. 227–232.
10. Walter Fogel, "The Emergency Employment Act in Los Angeles City and County," in *Case Studies of the Emergency Employment Act in Operation*, by the U.S. Senate Subcommittee on Employment, Poverty, and Migratory Labor, pp. 118, 120.
11. David P. Taylor, "Discrimination and Occupational Wage Differences in the Market for Unskilled Labor," *Industrial and Labor Relations Review* 21, no. 3 (April 1968): 375–390; see also Albert Rees and George P. Schultz, *Workers and Wages in an Urban Labor Market*, p. 162.
12. Fogel, *Mexican-Americans in Southwest Labor Markets*, pp. 130–136.
13. Ibid., pp. 128–130.
14. Schmidt, *Spanish Surnamed American Employment in the Southwest*, pp. 34–39.
15. Fogel, *Mexican-Americans in Southwest Labor Markets*, p. 129.
16. Schmidt, *Spanish Surnamed American Employment in the Southwest*, p. 32.
17. Jerelyn R. Lyle, "Factors Affecting the Job Status of Workers with Spanish Surnames," *Monthly Labor Review* 96, no. 4 (April 1973): 10–16. This finding must be regarded cautiously since the model which produced it has some shortcomings.
18. Fogel, *Mexican-Americans in Southwest Labor Markets*, p. 154.

5. THE RURAL ECONOMY

1. U.S. Bureau of the Census, "Persons of Spanish Surname,"*Census: 1970, Subject Reports*, PC(2)-1D, table 12, p. 81.
2. Leo Grebler, Joan W. Moore, and Ralph C. Guzman, *The Mexican-American People*, p. 90.
3. Ibid., pp. 8–9.
4. Vernon M. Briggs, Jr., *The Mexico–United States Border*.

5. U.S. Senate, Subcommittee on Migratory Labor of the Committee on Labor and Public Welfare, "Mexican Immigration and American Labor Demands," material prepared by Julian Samora and Jorge Bustamante, *Hearings on Migrant and Seasonal Farmworker Powerlessness*, 91st Cong., 1st and 2nd sess., pt. 7-B, April 15, 1970, pp. 4783–4784. [Paper presented at the Center for Migration Studies, Brooklyn College, March 1970.]
6. Ernesto Galarza, *Merchants of Labor*.
7. Carey McWilliams, *North from Mexico*, p. 267.
8. U.S. Department of Justice, Immigration and Naturalization Service, *Annual Report*, 1974, p. iii.
9. David S. North, *The Border Crossers*, pp. 31–33.
10. Michael Mallory, "Human Wave of Mexicans Splashes across Border," *National Observer*, October 16, 1971, p. 1.
11. Fred H. Schmidt and Kenneth Koford, "The Economic Condition of the Mexican-American," in *Mexican-Americans Tomorrow*, ed. Gus Tyler, pp. 81–106.
12. North, *The Border Crossers*, p. 72.
13. U.S. Commission on Civil Rights, Staff Report, "The Commuter on the United States–Mexican Border," *Hearings* in San Antonio, Texas, December 9–14, 1968, pp. 983–1006.
14. U.S. Commission on Civil Rights, *Hearings*.
15. David S. North, *Alien Workers*, p. 70.
16. Good Neighbor Commission of Texas, *Texas Migrant Labor Report, 1972*.
17. Anna-Strina Ericson, "The Impact of Commuters on the Mexican Border Area," *Monthly Labor Review* 93, no. 8 (August 1970): 18.
18. U.S. Senate, Subcommittee on Migratory Labor of the Committee on Labor and Public Welfare, *Hearings on Migrant and Seasonal Farmworker Powerlessness*, 91st Cong., 1st and 2nd sess., pt. 5-A, May 21, 1969, p. 2145.
19. U.S. House of Representatives, Subcommittee No. 1 of Committee on the Judiciary, "Statement of Sheldon Greene, General Counsel of California Rural Legal Assistance," *Hearings on Illegal Aliens*, 92nd Cong., 1st sess., pt. 1, June 21, 1971, p. 193.
20. U.S. Department of Justice, "A Program for Effective and Humane Action on Illegal Mexican Immigrants," *Final Report to the President of the United States by the Special Study Group on Illegal Immigrants from Mexico, U.S. Department of Justice*, January 15, 1973, p. 9; Good Neighbor Commission of Texas, *Texas Migrant Labor Report, 1972*, chap. 3, p. 9.
21. Lamar B. Jones, "Mexican-American Labor Problems in Texas," Ph.D. dissertation, University of Texas at Austin, 1965.

22. U.S. Senate, Subcommittee on Migratory Labor of the Committee on Labor and Public Welfare, "The Migratory Farm Labor Problem in the United States," *Report*, 91st Cong., 1st sess., February 1969, p. 5.
23. U.S. Senate, Subcommittee on Migratory Labor of the Committee on Labor and Public Welfare, "Testimony of Daniel Sturt, Director of the Rural Manpower Center, Michigan State University," *Hearings*, 91st Cong., 1st and 2nd sess., pt. 7-B, April 15, 1970, p. 4550.
24. Good Neighbor Commission of Texas, *Texas Migrant Labor Report, 1971*, summary section, p. 7.
25. Vernon M. Briggs, Jr., *Chicanos and Rural Poverty*, p. 64.
26. Ibid., p. 67.
27. Ibid., p. 49.
28. See Lamar B. Jones, "Labor and Management in California Agriculture, 1864–1964," *Labor History* 11 (Winter 1970): 23–40; and John D. Privett, "Agricultural Unionism among Chicanos," MBA thesis, University of Texas at Austin, 1971, chaps. 3, 4, and 5.
29. There are a number of accounts of the struggle by Chávez to gain recognition for his union. Among these are Mark Day, *Forty Acres*; Peter Matthiessen, *Sal Si Puedes*; and Jacques E. Levy, *César Chávez*.
30. U.S. Senate, Subcommittee on Migratory Labor of the Committee on Labor and Public Welfare, "Statement of César E. Chávez, Director, United Farm Workers Organizing Committee, AFL-CIO," *Hearings on Agricultural Labor Legislation*, 91st Cong., 1st sess., April 16, 1969, p. 23.
31. Briggs, *Chicanos and Rural Poverty*, pp. 56–60.
32. U.S. Senate, Subcommittee on Migratory Labor of the Committee on Labor and Public Welfare, "Testimony of Daniel Sturt," p. 4547.

6. PUBLIC POLICY NEEDS FOR FUTURE ECONOMIC OPPORTUNITY

1. George I. Sánchez, "History, Culture, and Education," in *La Raza*, p. 9.
2. Ernesto Galarza, "Mexicans in the Southwest: A Culture in Process," in *Plural Society in the Southwest*, ed. Edward H. Spicer and Raymond H. Thompson, p. 262.
3. Ibid., p. 267.
4. Fred Bonavita, "LULAC Votes to Ask Latin Minority Label," *Houston Post*, October 11, 1970, p. 1.

5. *Cisneros et al.* vs. *Corpus Christi Independent School District*, Southern District, Texas, Civil Action Number 68–C–95, June 4, 1970.
6. Ibid., pp. 9–10, fn. 31.
7. Carey McWilliams, *North from Mexico*, pp. 206–207.
8. Ibid.
9. Ibid., pp. 190–193; see also Leo Grebler, Joan W. Moore, and Ralph C. Guzman, *The Mexican-American People*, pp. 90–94.
10. Fred H. Schmidt, *Spanish Surnamed American Employment in the Southwest*, pp. 9–45.
11. U.S. Commission on Civil Rights, Mexican American Educational Series, *Study Report I*, p. 11.
12. Ibid., p. 12.
13. Ibid., p. 13.
14. Ibid., p. 12.
15. *Cisneros et al.* vs. *Corpus Christi Independent School District*.
16. U.S. Commission on Civil Rights, Mexican American Educational Series, *Study Report II*, pp. 41–42.
17. Vernon M. Briggs, Jr., *They Have the Power—We Have the People*.
18. Ibid., pp. 28–40, 94–95.
19. F. Ray Marshall and Vernon M. Briggs, Jr., *The Negro and Apprenticeship*.
20. Grebler, Moore, and Guzman, *The Mexican-American People*, p. 220.
21. Briggs, *They Have the Power—We Have the People*, p. 220.
22. Walter Fogel, "The Effects of Low Educational Attainment on Incomes: A Comparative Study of Selected Ethnic Groups," *Journal of Human Resources* 1, no. 2 (Fall 1966): 22–40. See also Vernon M. Briggs, Jr., *Negro Employment in the South*, vol. 1, *The Houston Labor Market*, chap. 2, which compares black and Chicano income and employment statistics. The figures for Chicanos were consistently more favorable than those for blacks despite the fact that the black educational attainment median was three years higher than that of Chicanos.

   And see Gilberto Cárdenas, "Patterns of Employment: The Mexican American Experience in Five Texas Cities." In this paper, the employment and income experiences of Chicanos and blacks are compared in five large labor-market areas in Texas. In every instance, Chicanos fared better than blacks.
23. Decision-Making Information, Inc., *MDT, Outcome Study*.
24. Fogel, "The Effects of Low Educational Attainment on Incomes," pp. 22–40.

25. See Gloria Stevenson, "The Job Corps Learns Spanish," *Manpower*, September 1972, pp. 7–15; "A Piece of the Action," *Manpower*, September 1971, pp. 8–14 (a printed dialogue between four Spanish-speaking Americans who discuss the manpower needs of their people); and Vernon M. Briggs, Jr., "Implications of Non-Institutional Considerations upon the Effectiveness of Manpower Programs for Chicanos," pp. 13–20.
26. U.S. Senate, Subcommittee on Migratory Labor of the Committee on Labor and Public Welfare, "Testimony of Daniel Sturt, Director of the Rural Manpower Center, Michigan State University," *Hearings*, 91st Cong., 1st and 2nd sess., pt. 7-B, April 15, 1970, p. 4548.
27. Vernon M. Briggs, Jr., *The Mexico–United States Border*, Studies in Human Resource Development, no. 2. See also Vernon M. Briggs, Jr., *Mexican Migration and the U.S. Labor Market*, Studies in Human Resource Development, no. 3.
28. For the specific policy needs, see Vernon M. Briggs, Jr., "Illegal Aliens: The Need for a More Restrictive Border Policy," *Social Science Quarterly* 56, no. 3 (December 1975): 477–484.

Bibliography

UNPUBLISHED MATERIAL

Briggs, Vernon M., Jr. "Implications of Non-Institutional Considerations upon the Effectiveness of Manpower Programs for Chicanos." Austin, Tex.: Center for the Study of Human Resources, 1973.
Cárdenas, Gilberto. "Patterns of Employment: The Mexican American Experience in Five Texas Cities." Austin: Center for the Study of Human Resources, University of Texas, 1973.
Decision-Making Information, Inc. *MDT, Outcome Study: Final Report*. Santa Ana, Calif.: Decision-Making Information, Inc., 1972.
Estrada, Leobardo F.; Hernández, José; and Alvírez, David. "Using Census Data to Study the Spanish Heritage Population of the United States." Paper presented at the Conference on the Demographic Study of the Mexican American Population sponsored by the Population Research Center and the Mexican American Center of the University of Texas at Austin, May 17, 1973.
Jones, Lamar B. "Mexican-American Labor Problems in Texas," Ph.D. dissertation, University of Texas at Austin, 1965.
King, Jonathan. "Social Inequality and Labor Force Participation." Ph.D. dissertation, University of California at Los Angeles, 1973.
Privett, John D. "Agricultural Unionism among Chicanos." MBA thesis, University of Texas at Austin, 1971.
Public Advocates, Inc. "California's and the Southwest's Largest Minority—One in Six a Chicano." San Francisco, January 1972.

GOVERNMENT DOCUMENTS

Briggs, Vernon M., Jr. *Negro Employment in the South*. Vol. 1, *The Houston Labor Market*. Manpower Research Monograph No. 23. Washington, D.C.: U.S. Government Printing Office, 1971.
———. *They Have the Power—We Have the People: An Equal Employment Opportunity Report*. Washington, D.C.: U.S. Commission on Equal Employment Opportunity, 1970.

Cisneros et al. vs. *Corpus Christi Independent School District*. South-
   ern District, Texas, Civil Action Number 68-C-95, June 4,
   1970.
Coleman, James, et al. *Equality of Educational Opportunity*.
   Washington, D.C.: U.S. Government Printing Office, 1966.
Confederación de La Raza Unida et al. vs. *George H. Brown, Director
   of the U.S. Census, et al.* Northern District, California, Civil
   Action Number C-71–2285, 1973.
Fogel, Walter. "The Emergency Employment Act in Los Angeles City
   and County." In *Case Studies of the Emergency Employment
   Act in Operation*, by the U.S. Senate Subcommittee on Em-
   ployment, Poverty, and Migratory Labor. Washington, D.C.:
   U.S. Government Printing Office, 1973.
Good Neighbor Commission of Texas. *Texas Migrant Labor Report,
   1971.* Austin: Good Neighbor Commission, 1972.
———. *Texas Migrant Labor Report, 1972.* Austin: Good Neighbor
   Commission, 1973.
———. *Texas Migrant Labor Report, 1973.* Austin: Good Neighbor
   Commission, 1974.
———. *Texas Migrant Labor Report, 1974.* Austin: Good Neighbor
   Commission, 1975.
———. *Texas Migrant Labor Report, 1975.* Austin: Good Neighbor
   Commission, 1976.
Hernández, Alfred J. "Civil Service and the Mexican American." In
   The Mexican American: A New Focus on Opportunity, by the
   Inter-Agency Committee on Mexican American Affairs.
   Washington, D.C.: U.S. Government Printing Office, 1967.
Schmidt, Fred H. *Spanish Surnamed American Employment in the
   Southwest*. Washington, D.C.: U.S. Government Printing
   Office, 1970.
U.S. Bureau of the Census. "American Indians." *Census of Population:
   1970. Subject Reports*. PC(2)-1F. Washington, D.C.: U.S.
   Government Printing Office, 1973.
———. *Census of Population: 1960*. Vol. 1, *Characteristics of the
   Population*. Pt. 1, *U.S. Summary*. Pt. 4, *Arizona*. Pt. 6,
   California. Pt. 7, *Colorado*. Pt. 33, *New Mexico*. Pt. 45, *Texas*.
   Washington, D.C.: U.S. Government Printing Office, 1963.
———. *Census of Population: 1970. Detailed Characteristics*. PC(1)-
   D1, *U.S. Summary*. PC(1)-D4, *Arizona*. PC(1)-D6, *California*.
   PC(1)-D7, *Colorado*. PC(1)-D33, *New Mexico*. PC(1)-D45,
   Texas. Washington, D.C.: U.S. Government Printing Office,
   1974.
———. *Census of Population: 1970. General Social and Economic
   Characteristics*. PC(1)-C1, *U.S. Summary*. PC(1)-C4, *Arizona*.

PC(1)-C6, *California*. PC(1)-C7, *Colorado*. PC(1)-C33, *New Mexico*. PC(1)-C45, *Texas*. Washington, D.C.: U.S. Government Printing Office, 1973.

————. *Census of Population: 1970. Number of Inhabitants*. PC(1)-A1, *U.S. Summary*. Washington, D.C.: U.S. Government Printing Office, 1973.

————. "Characteristics of the Population by Ethnic Origin: November 1969." *Current Population Reports*. P-20, no. 221. Washington, D.C.: U.S. Government Printing Office, April 1971.

————. *Employment Profiles of Selected Low-Income Areas*. PHC(3). Vols. 13 (Los Angeles, Calif.), 39 (San Diego, Calif.), 42 (Denver, Colo.), 48 (Phoenix, Ariz.), and 50 (San Antonio, Tex.). Washington, D.C.: U.S. Government Printing Office, 1972.

————. "Fertility Variations by Ethnic Origin: November 1969." *Current Population Reports*. P-20, no. 226, Washington, D.C.: U.S. Government Printing Office, November 1971.

————. "Households and Families, by Type: March 1972." *Current Population Reports*. P-20, no. 237. Washington, D.C.: U. S. Government Printing Office, 1973.

————. "Japanese, Chinese, and Filipinos in the United States." *Census of Population: 1970. Subject Reports*. PC(2)-1G. Washington, D.C.: U.S. Government Printing Office, 1973.

————. "Negro Population." *Census of Population: 1970. Subject Reports*. PC(2)-1B. Washington, D.C.: U.S. Government Printing Office, 1973.

————. "Persons of Spanish Ancestry." *Census of Population: 1970. Supplementary Report*. PC(S1)-30. Washington, D.C.: U.S. Government Printing Office, February 1973.

————. "Persons of Spanish Origin." *Census of Population: 1970. Subject Reports*. PC(2)-1C. Washington, D.C.: U.S. Government Printing Office, 1973.

————. "Persons of Spanish Origin in the United States: November 1969." *Current Population Reports*. P-20, no. 213. Washington, D.C.: U.S. Government Printing Office, 1971.

————. "Persons of Spanish Origin in the United States: March 1973." *Current Population Reports*. P-20, nos. 259 and 264. Washington, D.C.: U.S. Government Printing Office, January 1974.

————. "Persons of Spanish Surname." *Census of Population: 1960. Subject Reports*. PC(2)-1B. Washington, D.C.: U.S. Government Printing Office, 1963.

———. "Persons of Spanish Surname." *Census of Population: 1970. Subject Reports*. PC(2)-1D. Washington D.C.: U.S. Government Printing Office, 1973.

———. "Population Characteristics." *Current Population Reports*. P-20, no. 244. Washington, D.C.: U.S. Government Printing Office, December 1972.

———. "Selected Characteristics of Persons and Families of Mexican, Puerto Rican, and Other Spanish Origin: March 1971." *Current Population Reports*. P-20, no. 224. Washington, D.C.: U.S. Government Printing Office, October 1971.

———. "Selected Characteristics of Persons and Families of Mexican, Puerto Rican, and Other Spanish Origin: March 1972." *Current Population Reports*. P-20, no. 238. Washington, D.C.: U.S. Government Printing Office, July 1972.

———. "Voter Participation in November 1972." *Current Population Reports*. P-20, no. 224. Washington, D.C.: U.S. Government Printing Office, 1971.

U.S. Bureau of Labor Statistics. *Area Wage Survey*. Bulletin 1725–67. Washington, D.C.: U.S. Government Printing Office, 1973.

U.S. Commission on Civil Rights. Mexican American Educational Series. *Study Report I: Ethnic Isolation of Mexican Americans in the Public Schools of the Southwest*. Washington, D.C.: U.S. Government Printing Office, April 1971.

———. ———. *Study Report II: The Unfinished Education*. Washington, D.C.: U.S. Government Printing Office, October 1971.

———. ———. *Study Report III: The Excluded Student; Educational Practices Affecting Mexican Americans in the Southwest*. Washington, D.C.: U.S. Government Printing Office, August 1972.

———. Staff Report. "The Commuter on the United States–Mexican Border." *Hearings* in San Antonio, Texas, December 9–14, 1968, pp. 983–1006. Washington, D.C.: U.S. Government Printing Office, 1968.

U.S. Department of Justice. "A Program for Effective and Humane Action on Illegal Mexican Immigrants." *Final Report to the President of the United States by the Special Study Group on Illegal Immigrants from Mexico, U.S. Department of Justice*. January 15, 1973. Washington, D.C.: U.S. Department of Justice, 1973.

———. Immigration and Naturalization Service. *Annual Report*. Washington, D.C.: U.S. Government Printing Office, 1941–1975.

U.S. Department of Labor. *Manpower Report of the President, 1973*. Washington, D.C.: U.S. Government Printing Office, 1973.

U.S. House of Representatives. Subcommittee No. 1 of Committee on the Judiciary. "Statement of Sheldon Greene, General Counsel of California Rural Legal Assistance." *Hearings on Illegal Aliens.* 92nd Cong., 1st sess., pt. 1, June 21, 1971, pp. 188–195. Washington, D.C.: U.S. Government Printing Office, 1971.

U.S. Senate. Subcommittee on Migratory Labor of the Committee on Labor and Public Welfare, "Mexican Immigration and American Labor Demands." Material prepared by Julian Samora and Jorge Bustamante. *Hearings on Migrant and Seasonal Farmworker Powerlessness.* 91st Cong., 1st and 2nd sess., pt. 7-B, April 15, 1970, pp. 4783–4821. Washington, D.C.: U.S. Government Printing Office, 1971.

———. ———. *Hearings on Migrant and Seasonal Farmworker Powerlessness.* 91st Cong., 1st and 2nd sess., pt. 5-A, May 21, 1969, p. 2145. Washington, D.C.: U.S. Government Printing Office, 1970.

———. ———. "The Migratory Farm Labor Problem in the United States." *Report.* 91st Cong., 1st sess., February 1969. Washington, D.C.: U.S. Government Printing Office, 1969.

———. ———. "Statement of César E. Chávez, Director, United Farm Workers Organizing Committee, AFL-CIO." *Hearings on Agricultural Labor Legislation.* 91st Cong., 1st sess., April 16, 1969, pp. 22–23. Washington, D.C.: U.S. Government Printing Office, 1971.

———. ———. "Testimony of Daniel Sturt, Director of the Rural Manpower Center, Michigan State University." *Hearings.* 91st Cong., 1st and 2nd sess., pt. 7-B, April 15, 1970, pp. 4527–4578. Washington, D.C.: U.S. Government Printing Office, 1971.

U.S. Tariff Commission. *Economic Factors Affecting the Use of Items 807.00 and 806.30 of the Tariff Schedules of the U.S.* Washington, D.C.: U.S. Government Printing Office, 1970.

BOOKS AND ARTICLES

Acuña, Rodolfo. *Occupied America: The Chicano's Struggle toward Liberation.* San Francisco: Canfield Press, 1972.

Bakerville, Tim. "The Border Game." *West Magazine, Los Angeles Times*, September 17, 1972.

Bloom, Gordon F., and Northrup, Herbert R. *Economics of Labor Relations.* 7th ed. Homewood, Ill.: Richard D. Irwin, 1973.

Bonavita, Fred. "LULAC Votes to Ask Latin Minority Label." *Houston Post*, October 11, 1970.

Briggs, Vernon M., Jr. *Chicanos and Rural Poverty*. Baltimore, Md.:
    Johns Hopkins Press, 1973.
————. "Illegal Aliens: The Need for a More Restrictive Border Policy."
    Social Science Quarterly 56, no. 3 (December 1975): 477–484.
————. *Mexican Migration and the U.S. Labor Market*. Studies in
    Human Resource Development, no. 3. Austin, Tex.: Center for
    Study of Human Resources and Bureau of Business Research,
    1975.
————. *The Mexico–United States Border: Public Policy and Chicano
    Economic Welfare*. Studies in Human Resource Development,
    no. 2. Austin, Tex.: Center for Study of Human Resources and
    Bureau of Business Research, 1974.
Bullock, Paul. *Aspirations vs. Opportunity: Careers in the Inner City*.
    Ann Arbor: Institute of Labor and Industrial Relations, Univer-
    sity of Michigan–Wayne State University, 1973.
————. "Employment Problems of the Mexican-American." In *Mexi-
    can Americans in the United States*, edited by John H. Burma.
    Cambridge, Mass.: Schenkman Publishing Co., 1970. [Origi-
    nally published in *Industrial Relations* 3 (May 1964): 37–50.]
Crossland, Fred E. *Minority Access to College: A Ford Foundation
    Report*. New York: Schocken Books, 1971.
Day, Mark. *Forty Acres: César Chávez and the Farm Workers*. New
    York: Praeger Publishers, 1971.
Ericson, Anna-Strina. "The Impact of Commuters on the Mexican
    Border Area." *Monthly Labor Review* 93, no. 8 (August 1970):
    18–27.
Fogel, Walter. "The Effects of Low Educational Attainment on In-
    comes: A Comparative Study of Selected Ethnic Groups."
    Journal of Human Resources 1, no. 2 (Fall 1966): 22–40.
————. "Job Gains of Mexican-American Men." *Monthly Labor Re-
    view* 91, no. 10 (October 1968): 22–27.
————. *Mexican-Americans in Southwest Labor Markets*. Los
    Angeles: University of California at Los Angeles, 1967. [Mexi-
    can American Study Project.]
————. "Summary Report VI: Los Angeles City and County." In
    Emergency Employment Act: The PEP Generation, edited by
    Sar Levitan and Robert Taggart, pp. 135–160. Salt Lake City,
    Utah: Olympus Publishing Co., 1974.
Forbes, Jack D. *Mexican-Americans: A Handbook for Educators*.
    Berkeley, Calif.: Far West Laboratory for Educational Research
    and Development, 1970.
Fuller, Roden. "Occupations of the Mexican-Born Population in Texas,
    New Mexico, and Arizona, 1900–1920." *Journal of the Ameri-
    can Statistical Association* 23, no. 161 (March 1928): 64–67.

Galarza, Ernesto. *Merchants of Labor: The Mexican Bracero Story*. Charlotte, N.C.: McNally & Lofting, 1964.

———. "Mexicans in the Southwest: A Culture in Process." In *Plural Society in the Southwest*, edited by Edward H. Spicer and Raymond H. Thompson. New York: Interbook, 1972.

Grebler, Leo; Moore, Joan W.; and Guzman, Ralph C. *The Mexican-American People: The Nation's Second Largest Minority*. New York: Free Press, 1970.

Greenwood, Noel. "Five-Million-Dollar Bilingual Education Bill Signed." *Los Angeles Times*, December 21, 1972.

Hammerman, Herbert, "Minority Workers in Construction Referral Unions." *Monthly Labor Review* 95, no. 5 (May 1972): 17–26.

Horgan, Paul. *Great River: The Rio Grande in North American History*. Vol. 1, *The Indians and Spain*. Vol. 2, *Mexico and the United States*. New York: Minerva Press, 1954.

Humphrey, N. D. "Employment Patterns of Mexicans in Detroit." *Monthly Labor Review* 61, no. 5 (November 1945): 913–923.

"Immigration: Revolving Door." *Newsweek Magazine*, July 23, 1973, p. 24.

Jones, Lamar B. "Labor and Management in California Agriculture, 1864–1964." *Labor History* 11 (Winter 1970): 23–40.

Levy, Jacques E. *César Chávez: Autobiography of La Causa*. New York: W.W. Norton & Co., 1975.

Los Angeles Times, 1971–1974.

Lyle, Jerelyn R. "Factors Affecting the Job Status of Workers with Spanish Surname." *Monthly Labor Review* 96, no. 4 (April 1973): 10–16.

McWilliams, Carey. *North from Mexico*. New York: Greenwood Press, 1968.

Mallory, Michael. "Human Wave of Mexicans Splashes across Border." *National Observer*, October 16, 1971.

Marshall, F. Ray, and Briggs, Vernon M., Jr. *The Negro and Apprenticeship*. Baltimore, Md.: Johns Hopkins Press, 1967.

Matthiessen, Peter. *Sal Si Puedes: César Chávez and the New American Revolution*. New York: Random House, 1970.

Moore, Joan. *Mexican Americans*. Englewood Cliffs, N.J.: Prentice-Hall, 1970.

North, David S. *Alien Workers: A Study of the Labor Certification Program*. Washington, D.C.: Trans Century Corporation, 1971.

———. *The Border Crossers: People Who Live in Mexico and Work in the United States*. Washington, D.C.: Trans Century Corporation, 1970.

"A Piece of the Action." *Manpower*, September 1971, pp. 8–14.

Posten, Dudley L., Jr., and Alvírez, David. "On the Cost of Being a Mexican-American Worker." *Social Science Quarterly* 53, no. 4 (March 1973): 697–709.

Ramírez, Henry M. "America's Spanish Speaking: A Profile." *Manpower*, September 1972, pp. 30–34.

Rees, Albert, and Shultz, George P. *Workers and Wages in an Urban Labor Market*. Chicago: University of Chicago Press, 1970.

Samora, Julian. "Mexican Immigration." In *Mexican-Americans Tomorrow*, edited by Gus Tyler, pp. 60–80. Albuquerque: University of New Mexico Press, 1975.

———, and Lamana, Richard. *Mexican Americans in a Midwest Metropolis: A Study of East Chicago*. [Mexican American Study Project.] Los Angeles: University of California at Los Angeles, 1967.

Sánchez, George I. "History, Culture, and Education." In *La Raza: Forgotten Americans*. Notre Dame, Ind.: University of Notre Dame Press, 1966.

Schmidt, Fred H., and Koford, Kenneth. "The Economic Condition of the Mexican-American." In *Mexican-Americans Tomorrow*, edited by Gus Tyler, pp. 81–106. Albuquerque: University of New Mexico Press, 1975.

Stevenson, Gloria. "The Job Corps Learns Spanish." *Manpower*, September 1972, pp. 7–15.

Taylor, David P. "Discrimination and Occupational Wage Differences in the Market for Unskilled Labor." *Industrial and Labor Relations Review* 21, no. 3 (April 1968): 375–390.

Taylor, Paul S. *Mexican Labor in the United States: Chicago and the Calumet Region*. Berkeley: University of California Press, 1932.

Williams, J. Allen, Jr.; Beeson, Peter G.; and Johnson, David R. "Some Factors Associated with Income among Mexican-Americans." *Social Science Quarterly* 53, no. 4 (March 1973): 710–715.

Young, Anne M. "The High School Class of 1972: More at Work, Fewer in College." *Monthly Labor Review* 96, no. 6 (June 1973): 26–32.

Index

Agricultural policy, 80
Agriculture, U.S. Department of, 87
Alien registration card (i.e., Form I-151): counterfeit issuance of, 15. *See also* "Green carders"
American Civil Liberties Union (A.C.L.U.), 15–16
American GI Forum, 38
American Indians, 21, 93, 98
Anglos: earnings of, 65–67; female, 32, 34; income of, 43; use of the word, xiii
Apprenticeship Information Reports, 39
Apprenticeship training, 39
Arizona, xiv, 32–33; college graduates in, 20–21; incomes in, 49
Asian Americans, 45, 93
Austin, Texas, 58

Bañuelos, Ramona, 16
Bilingual education, 21
Birthrate, 8
Blacks: and college education, 21; and income comparison, 48. *See also* Negroes
Border crossers, 14–17. *See also* Commuters; "Green carders"; and "White carders"
Border Industrialization Program, 41–42
Border Patrol, 11–12
Bracero program, 12, 81–82; and Public Law 45 and 78, 81–82
Briggs, Jr., Vernon M., 87

Brown vs. *Board of Education* (1954), 95
Bullock, Paul, 23
Bustamante, Jorge, 81

California, xii–xiv, 10, 17–18; bilingual education in, 22; college graduates in, 20–21; discrimination in, 97–98; earnings in, 65–67, 72; educational gap in, 20; foreign born in, 17; illegal immigrants in, 16; income in, 46–48, 61; labor force in, 26, 30–31, 33; and legal immigrants from Mexico, 13; participation of, in manpower programs, 38; poverty in, 52; schooling and income in, 47–48, 56; unemployment in, 34; welfare in, 52
California Agricultural Relations Act (1975), 89–91
California Rural Legal Assistance, 85
Californios, 10
Census, U.S. Bureau of the, 5–6, 9, 22, 78
Census of Population: 1960, 18, 34–36; income and education in, 54
Census of Population: 1970, xi–xiii, 18; family size in, 8; income and education in, 54; migration patterns in, 17; poverty in, 91; rural population in, 78; school completions in, 20, 39; urbanization in, 18

Census of Population and Housing: 1970, 40
Central America, 9
Central Valley of California, 94
Chávez, César, 89
Chicago, Illinois, 17, 19, 63, 70; migration from Mexico to, 48
Chicanas, xiii; comparison of, with black women, 65; discouragement of, from competing with males, 31–32; fertility of, 7–8; income of, 49, 60; labor force and, 31, 33; nonparticipation of, in labor force, 31
Chicanos, xi, xiii–xiv; and discrimination, 95–96; and geographic mobility, 17–18; income of, 48–49, 51; as largest minority in Southwest, 5; and stamp of inferiority, 4; and urbanization, 18
Chinese Exclusion Act (1882), 81
Civil Rights Act (1964), 102
Coleman report, 55. See also Equality of Educational Opportunity (1966)
Colorado, xiv, 13, 17; Chicano population of, 9; income in, 48–51; labor force in, 32; school completions in, 20; unemployment in, 36
Commission on Civil Rights, U.S., 19–21, 84, 86, 98
Commuters, 58, 82, 86, 92. See also "Green carders"
Conquistadores, 3, 11
Corpus Christi, Texas, 95, 98, 103
Cuban Refugee Program, 14
Cubans, 8, 45
Cultural differences, 20, 22–25, 33

Delgado vs. The Bastrop Independent School District (1948), 98
Denver, Colorado, 48; metropolitan area of, 94
Detroit, Michigan, 48, 63
Dictionary of Occupational Titles, 71
Discrimination, 18, 23, 38, 43, 55, 58, 70, 95, 101; in housing, 97; and human capital effects, 56–58; in industrial unions, 99–100; informal, 99; job position and, 74; as overt segregation, 97–98; in union practices, 39, 97, 99, 102

Eastern Hemisphere, 11
Educational disadvantages, 19–22
Educational opportunity, 19–20
El Paso, Texas, 11, 19
Emergency Employment Act (1971), 39, 68
Employment and Training Administration. See Manpower Administration
English, 9
English as a second language, 21–22
Equal Employment Opportunity Commission, U.S. (EEOC), 39–40, 71, 74, 102; and Houston hearings, 98–99
Equality of Educational Opportunity (1966), 55
Ethnic isolation, 20

Fair Labor Standards Act (1968), 88
Farah, Inc., 42
Florida, 8, 10
Fogel, Walter, 55, 70–71
Fraudulent documents, 15

Gadsden Purchase (1853), 80

Galarza, Ernesto, 82, 94
Gentlemen's Agreement (1907),
  81
Great Northern Railroad, 63
"Green carders", 83–85. *See also*
  Commuters
Greene, Sheldon, 85
Guadalupe Hidalgo, Treaty of
  (1848), 4, 80

Health, Education and Welfare,
  U.S. Department of, 38
Hidalgo County, Texas, 19
Hispanos, 10
Houston, Texas, 18, 48, 58, 103
Human capital, 56, 58

Idaho, 10, 17
Illegal immigration, 14–17, 57,
  86; and need for tight border
  policy, 103–104
Illinois, 10, 12–13; legal immigrants from Mexico to, 17;
  income in, 48
Immigration Act (1965), 84
Immigration and Nationality Act
  (1952), 12
Immigration and Naturalization
  Act (1924), 11
Immigration and Naturalization
  Service (INS), 15, 82
Income and earnings: and age, 53;
  and changes over time, 59–61;
  and educational differences,
  53–57; and family income,
  43–46; and individual differences, 49; and intergeneration-
  al change, 49–51; male and
  female comparison of, 60;
  regional differences in, 46–48
International Brotherhood of
  Teamsters (independent), 89,
  90
International Longshoremen's

Association (AFL-CIO), 100
Iowa, 17

Japan, 81
Japanese Americans, 45
Job Corps, 102
Justice, U.S. Department of, 91

Kansas, 10, 17, 22
Kansas City, Missouri, 63
King, Jonathan, 56

Labor, U.S. Department of, 21,
  38, 96
Labor certification, 84
Labor force, 26–30; participation,
  30–34
Landrum-Griffin Act (1959), 89
Laredo, Texas, 58
League of United Latin American
  Citizens, 38
Legal immigrants from Mexico,
  12, 49; characteristics of, 13–
  14
Legal immigration from Mexico,
  as compared to illegal immigra-
  tion, 80
Los Angeles, California, 6, 15,
  19, 24, 48; metropolitan area
  of, 94; textile and apparel in-
  dustry in, 68
Los Angeles County, California, 6

McWilliams, Carey, 4, 62, 96
Manpower Administration, U.S.,
  36, 40
Manpower Development and
  Training Act (1962), 102
*Manpower Report of the Presi-
  dent: 1973*, 27, 34
Manpower training, 30, 36–40,
  87, 94. *See also* Operation SER
Méndez et al. vs. *Westminster
  School District* (1945), 98

Mexican Americans, xiii. *See also* Chicanos or Chicanas

Mexican American Study Project, 20, 24, 80

Mexican farm labor program. *See* Bracero program

Mexican origin, xi, xii–xiv, 5, 62; fertility of women of, 8; income of families of, 43–44, 48, 57; population increase of persons of, 8

Mexican War (1846–1848): antecedents of, 3; atrocities of, 3; as war of imperialism, 4

Mexico: border of, with United States, 19, 41–42; and commuters, 83; cost of living in, 84; and cultural ties, 9–10; and illegal entry to U.S., 41–42; and immigration to U.S., 10, 12, 14, 17, 41, 49, 79, 93; wage differences between U.S. and, 41; and war with U.S., 3

Mexico, Gulf of, 10

Michigan, 10, 17, 22, 48

Migratory farm labor, 86; U.S. Senate Subcommittee on Migratory Labor of the Committee on Labor and Public Welfare, 86–87

Mondale, Walter F., 86, 91, 103

Morrill Act (1862), 93

National Labor Relations Act (1935), 88–89

National Migrant Program, 102

National Origins Act (1924), 83

Nebraska, 17, 22

Negroes: apprenticeship participation of, 40; earnings of, 65–67; income of, 43–44, 51–53; labor-market information on, 34; median age of, 8; occupa-

tional patterns of, 63. *See also* Blacks

Nevada, 10

New Jersey, 8

New Mexico, xiv, 17; Chicano population of, 9; college graduates in, 21; income in, 51; labor-force participation in, 30, 33; manpower programs in, 38; original settlers in, 10; urbanization in, 18

"Newness hypothesis," 50

New York, 8, 10, 13

North, David S., 83, 84

Oakland, California, 19

Office of Economic Opportunity, U.S., 38

Office of Federal Contract Compliance, U.S., 71

Ohio, 10, 22, 63

Operation SER, 38–39, 102–103

Orange County, California, 19, 48, 98

Oregon, 17

Population Commission of California, 6

President's Committee on Opportunities for Spanish Speaking People, 24

Public Employment Program, 39

Public Law 45 and 78, 81–82. *See also* Bracero program

Puerto Ricans, 21, 44, 70; and higher education, 21; residence patterns of, 21

"Queuing theory", 68–69, 71–72

Railroad construction, 62

Ramírez, Henry M., 24

Rio Grande, 10, 94

Riverside County, California, 19

Rock Island Railroad, 63
Rodino, Peter W., 86
Rural economy, 78–92; income in, 46
Russian origin, 44

Salt River valley, Arizona, 94
Samora, Julian, 81
San Antonio, Texas, 19, 24, 58, 84
San Bernardino County, California, 19
Sánchez, George I., 93
San Diego, California, 19
San Francisco, California, 19, 48; basin area of, 94
San Jose, California, 19
Santa Fe, New Mexico, 9
San Ysidro, California, 15
Schmidt, Fred H., 71
Scott Winfield, 3
Servicemen's Readjustment Act (1944), 93
Slavery, 3, 15
South America, 9
Southern Pacific Railroad, 63
South Texas, 41, 48, 58, 68, 86. See also Texas
Spain, 9
Spanish-heritage Americans, 93
Spanish language–Spanish surname, xi–xiv, 5, 19
Spanish origin, xiii–xiv, 10, 70; as foreign born, 17; income of, 44; schooling and income of, 56
Spanish-speaking Americans: labor-market experience of, 27; work experience of, 34
Spanish surname, xi–xiv, 5, 18; age and income of, 53; immigration of, 57; income of, 43–49, 60–61; manpower programs of, 36; median age of, 8; poverty of, 51–53; school completion of, 20

Taft-Hartley Act (1947), 89
Tariff regulation, U.S., 41
Taylor, David, 70
Texas, xiv, 11, 17, 95; annexed by United States, 3; Chicano population of, 9, 18; discrimination in, 97–98; earnings in, 65–67, 72; educational gap in, 20; labor-force participation in, 26, 30–33; legal immigrants from Mexico in, 13; poverty in, 52–53; Republic of, 3; unemployment in, 34. See also South Texas
Texas Good Neighbor Commission, 87

Undercount problems, 5
Unemployment, 21, 34–36
Unemployment compensation, 88
United Farm Workers of America (UFW), 89, 90
United States, 11, 97; commuters to, 84–85; immigration to, 79; wage differences of, with Mexico, 41
Utah, 10

Vocational training, 39, 56

Wage standardization, 74–75
Washington, 10, 17
Welfare, 52
Western Hemisphere, 11
"White carders," 84. See also Commuters
Wisconsin, 10

Young, Anne M., 21